ANTHONY DE MELLO

Anand Nayak

Anthony de Mello
HIS LIFE AND HIS SPIRITUALITY

the columba press

First published in 2007 by
the columba press
55A Spruce Avenue, Stillorgan Industrial Park,
Blackrock, Co Dublin

Cover by Bill Bolger
Origination by The Columba Press
Printed in Ireland by ColourBooks Ltd, Dublin

ISBN 978 1 85607 560 2

Copyright © 2007, Anand Nayak

Table of Contents

Foreword 7

CHAPTER ONE
Who is Anthony de Mello? 10
    Early education 12
    Becoming a Jesuit 13
    Training in psychology 20
    Missionary life 23
    Retreat master and spiritual counsellor 24
    Discovery of Indian masters 27
    Institute for Pastoral Counselling and Spirituality 34
    Sadhana Institute 39
    Friends and detractors 45
    The last pictures 49

CHAPTER TWO
Spiritual teachings of Father Anthony de Mello 55
    An outline of Father de Mello's spirituality 58
    1. Happiness is the goal.
        But, instead, many experience only suffering. 59
        Acquired happiness 59
        Real happiness 63
    2. The cause of suffering is attachment;
        that is, happiness sought through conditions. 64
    3. There is a way out: detachment through discernment. .. 66
        What is detachment? 67
        Discernment 68
        Discernment through awareness 71
    4. Happiness is freedom. 75
    Concluding remarks: Spirituality without Jesus Christ? .. 77

CHAPTER THREE
Father Anthony de Mello's Spirituality
    against the background of the Vatican's Notification .. 83
    1. Father Anthony de Mello and his works 84
        Two works wrongly attributed to Father de Mello .. 85
    2. The positive features of the teaching of Father de Mello:
        Oriental wisdom 89
    3. Within the boundaries of Christian spirituality 91

4. Acceptable teachings	93
5. Progressive distancing from the Christian faith	95
6. Silence as the great revelation	97
7. The Heart and the void	100
8. Awareness, awakening and holiness	103
9. The Approach of the Notification	110
10. Personal nature of God ignored	112
11. The radical or exaggerated apophatism	120
12. Scripture as a road-sign	136
13. Religions	140
14. Truth and fanaticism	143
15. Jesus Christ	150
Jesus as master alongside others	158
The only difference between Jesus and others	159
Jesus is not recognised as the Son of God	163
Christ's presence in the Eucharist is but a symbol	165
16. Final destiny: Dissolving into the impersonal God	166
17. Time and destiny after death	172
18. Evil, ethics and morality; sin and repentance	179
19. Church has lost the authority to teach	189
20. Danger	198

CHAPTER FOUR

Is Father Anthony de Mello a danger to the Catholic Faith?	200
Reactions to the Vatican Notification	200
Pastoral guidelines of the bishops in India	201
The reaction of the Jesuits in India	202
Reactions over the world	205
Father Carlos Vallés	208
To whom is Father de Mello a danger?	209
A Prophet for our times	210
Father de Mello: A Healer	210
Father de Mello and the future of the Catholic Church	211

Foreword

The publication of the *Notification concerning the writings of Father Anthony de Mello, S.J.,* issued by Vatican's Congregation for the Doctrine of the Faith on June 24 1998, was a shock to Christians, as well as to non-Christians, all over the world. People, who had known Father Anthony de Mello (1931-1987) personally or through his writings, were at loss as to why a solemn notification was needed to warn Catholics against a person in whom they had recognised a healthy sanctity rather than a danger to the faith. Others who did not know Father de Mello wondered why Rome should interfere with the writings of an Indian Jesuit far away in India. Numerous reviews and newspapers reported the event but, strangely enough, not one paper nor one serious writer rose up in defence of the Vatican text.

Furthermore, the *Notification* was sent to all the bishops with a letter annexed to it, whose contents were not to be divulged to the public. It was written in clear terms by the Prefect of the Congregation for the Doctrine of the Faith, Joseph Cardinal Ratzinger, ordering the bishops to intercept the sale of Father de Mello's books and to see that his teachings did not circulate in their dioceses. Most of the bishops, again at a loss to evaluate the real danger, fulfilled their duty by bringing the document to the notice of the public without, however, giving their own personal comments on the matter. The Jesuit headquarters in Rome were particularly silent on the issue, leaving the whole matter to the Jesuits in India.

The *Notification* to this day has not brought any perceptible results. The church in India and the Jesuits there have not taken any steps to forbid the reading of Father de Mello's books. On the contrary, they have recommended them to be read but with a certain discernment. Surprisingly, however, they have not taken any perceptible action to defend their brother, probably not to further excite the Vatican authorities who have already become apprehensive of the theologians in India. They seem to be resigned, out of frustration, to the repeated interventions from Rome which, in their opinion, betray an incapacity to understand and justly evaluate what happens in the church in India.

If Father de Mello's books have, in fact, disappeared from the shelves of some pious bookshops, sales have increased in others if only because of the Vatican's warnings against them. Some shrewd booksellers have even attached red warning labels – similar to those on cigarette packets – that reading the books may be dangerous to the (spiritual) health of the reader. Naturally, this action has boosted sales. The Vatican's action seems to have succeeded in silencing the publishers of Father de Mello's books, the Gujarat Sahitya Prakash. When I approached them about the publication of this book, my offer was politely declined.

The present study does not question the right of the church to issue warnings for the good of the faithful, nor does it question what the teaching body of the church determines as being right or wrong. Its sole purpose is to point out to the public that the writers of this *Notification* have produced a text riddled with mistakes and based on a faulty comprehension and interpretation of the texts of Father de Mello. Of the texts adduced to warn of the danger, there is not one that can be rightly used against Father de Mello. This is doubtlessly a serious matter. For those who sit so close, morally, but also physically, to the seat of infallibility cannot venture to destroy the name and fame of an illustrious spiritual master with a document riddled with faults. In that way, the *Notification* seems to be self-destructive and calls for an earnest revision of the question of Father Anthony de Mello's writings.

The study of the document is made primarily in chapter three of this work. To make the reading easier and to get hold of some clear landmarks in a dense forest of ideas, I have taken the liberty of presenting the Roman text in divisions and under subtitles that are not in the original text, which is continuous and difficult to read. The official text of the document is available on the web at:

http://www.ewtn.com/library/CURIA/CDFDEMEL.HTM

This study has been brewing in my heart ever since the publication of the *Notification*. Although the substance of it was worked out in my office at the University of Fribourg,

FOREWORD

Switzerland, I have the joy of terminating it on this day in my family apartment at Bandra, in Mumbai, India, only a few feet away from St Peter's Church where Father de Mello rests in peace.

Anand Nayak
6 April 2006

CHAPTER ONE

Who is Anthony de Mello?

Although Father Anthony de Mello's books have become highly popular all over the world, very little is known to his readers of his life and person. Many, for example, do not know that he was an Indian from India. I attempt here to draw a picture of his life so that the readers might get a better background of his writings and assess more justly the position which the Vatican Curia has taken towards him and towards his work. None of his Jesuit companions who knew him personally, nor his close and intimate friends, have attempted so far to write his biography. The work of the Jesuit Carlos Vallés, *Unencumbered by Baggage: Tony de Mello, A prophet for our times*, appeared in 1987 (Gujarat Sahitya Prakash, Anand), a few months after de Mello's death. It is not a biography but a good description of the spiritual master that he was for many. Almost a decade later, in 1995, a number of his disciples and friends collected anecdotes from their experience of their spiritual master in a book entitled *We Heard the Bird Sing: Interacting with Anthony de Mello, S.J.* (from the same publishing house). Sometime back his brother Bill de Mello published on the Internet (http://users.tpg.com.au/adsligol/tony/ or http://www.spiritwalk.org/demello.htm#biography) a short but impressive account of his early life, with several family photos. What I write here is only an attempt at a brief biographical introduction to the study of his writings.

Anthony de Mello was born on 4 September 1931 at Santa Cruz, a suburb of the city of Bombay which is now known as Mumbai. His mother Luisa Castellino (1906-1980) and his father Frank de Mello (1902-1968) were both of Indian descent and natives of Goa.

Goa, a region situated on the West coast of India, was a Portuguese colony since 1510. In 1961 the Indian army re-conquered it and annexed it to the Republic of India in which it has now the status of a state. Goan Christians have Portuguese names because the missionary policy of the Catholic Church then, and until recently, required that the new converts be given the name of a canonised saint. At their baptism, the local Portuguese landlord gave them his own Portuguese family name. The first name later took an English form because Goans entertained closer relationships with the British colonials. They were given better job opportunities in the public service, not only in the British colonial India but also elsewhere in the surrounding colonial territories. They then learnt English and adapted English living habits. After India's independence in 1947 and after the annexing of Goa, many of them emigrated to English-speaking countries where they strive to maintain a Goan identity, marked by English, Indian and Goan cultural traits.

Anthony de Mello's family spoke English at home and lived more attuned to a Western atmosphere, although his mother Luisa insisted on wearing a sari and respecting the traditional Indian social traditions. Since Frank was an employee of the Indian Railways, the family lived in the railway colony of Santa Cruz. These colonies in India were, at that time, marked by an Anglo-Indian culture. People of Indian origin living there often referred to themselves as 'Anglo-Indians'. Goans, too, were welcome in this community, which projected the spirit of a micro-community, the 'Great Indian Railway Family'.

Anthony, or 'Tony,' as he was called at home, grew up in this peculiar Indian-English atmosphere. He was the eldest child, followed by Grace (1933), Marina (1937) and Bill (1944). In 1952 the family moved to Bandra, another suburb of Bombay, where they could avail themselves of a more spacious house and better educational facilities. After long service, Frank quit the railways and joined the Associated Cement Company, from which he retired a few years later. Today, Grace and Bill live in Australia, and Marina has immigrated to Canada.

Tony's early life (I here follow Bill de Mello's biography), was steeped in the Catholic religion, which meant, at that time, daily Mass and taking an active part in all church services: Benediction of the Blessed Sacrament, Way of the Cross, weekly confessions, daily rosary and litany at home, observation of nine First Fridays, novenas, indulgences and so on. Tony, the pious and exemplary child of the family, had freely and gladly embraced this practice of the traditional Catholicism, developing within himself a strong and rigid moralising attitude which he, as he grew up, did not fail to impose on his younger sisters and brother. The church, dogmas and discipline were the most important things in his life. His father, Frank, was a soft man who cared very much for the family and its well being, while his mother, Luisa, had a very strong personality. She believed and practised her faith but never sheepishly followed the dictates of the church authorities. Thus, when she died of cancer in 1980, she requested that she be cremated. Cremation was a taboo at that time in the Catholic community. But Tony, by that time a renowned Jesuit priest, decided against the practice of the local church. He held the funeral celebration at home and then proceeded with the cremation. Later on, the family requested the parish priest of St Peter's, their parish, to allot them a plot in the church cemetery to bury the ashes of Luisa. But the request was promptly and sternly refused.

Early Education
Tony completed his early education at St Stanislaus High School, Bandra, a prestigious Jesuit school in Bombay. At that time, Spanish Jesuits – more precisely Catalans – were active in Bombay. The Jesuit Province of Barcelona sent its members to take up work in mission stations and to look after the Christian education of their flock. Some of these Jesuits were highly gifted intellectuals and humanists. They built schools and colleges in Bombay that have trained generations of eminent men. Their choice to train the elite (who were also the rich) of Bombay is now slowly being given up by the newer generations of Indian Jesuits in favour of the poor and the downtrodden, without, however, lowering the educational standards.

The Spanish Jesuits were models in life for the Catholic boys of their schools. Tony came to admire them and grew up in their shadow. Academically, he was an exceptionally bright student, gifted in languages and endowed with fine human and social qualities. Living in Bombay, it was necessary to learn a variety of languages. Besides English, he could speak two Indian languages fluently: the provincial language Marathi and the 'everyman's' language in Bombay City, Hindi.

Given the ease with which Tony could excel in academics, his parents expected him to pursue higher education at the university and to choose a financially profitable career. Those post-war days being full of uncertainty, his father hinted that he should take a secure job on the railways. But, by then, Tony had made clear to his parents his wish to join the Jesuits. His parents did not pay attention to it at first, thinking that it was a passing fervour created by the Jesuits whom he admired at school. They insisted on his responsibility to meet the family's financial needs. Moreover, their intelligent and saintly son was not altogether averse to life's pleasures and ambitions. Bill recounts an anecdote in his biography: 'My parents knew that Tony also had a romantic side. When he was quite young, he told a cousin of ours that some day he would marry her and that he would take all the stars in the sky and make her a wedding dress. She never failed to remind him jokingly of his promise, even years after he had joined the Jesuits, and she was married with children.'(cf website cited above)

A few months before the end of his high school education, Tony attended a career-counselling course which helped him make the final and definite decision to join the Jesuits. However his mother suggested a compromise: let him be a secular priest, so that he could be more available to his family, since the Jesuits, being religious, were not allowed to visit their families regularly and frequently. But Tony was adamant about his choice and, when his parents realised that no argument would make him change his mind, they yielded to his wish. He joined the Jesuit noviciate, Vinayalaya, situated not far from the family house in the Bombay suburb of Andheri, on 1 July 1947, at the tender age of 16 years.

Becoming a Jesuit
The making of a Jesuit is a slow and uneventful process. The formation period in those days lasted about 15 years. Nothing extraordinary happened during those years, since the whole training was pre-set by rules and regulations to which the young

man was required to surrender, as to the Will of God, his life and its destiny. Individuality and personal variations were not easily permitted. A Jesuit ripened slowly and steadily, like an apple on the tree, one among many. The Jesuit formation of Tony lasted longer than usual, for 18 years.

The noviciate, according to the Jesuit formation programme, is a two-year intense introduction to spiritual life, supposedly the most important part of the Jesuit's spiritual training. There, the worldly man is moulded into a spiritual person. The house Vinayalaya meant 'the house for Vinaya'. I do not know if the Spanish Jesuits had consciously chosen the word *vinaya*, the Buddhist word for 'rules'. There was certainly no special interest shown in Buddhism there, for the entire attention was laid on modelling one's life on the rules given by the founder, Ignatius of Loyola (1491-1556). Probably the name was chosen to describe the Jesuit formation house in an Indian term to the largely non-Christian population of the locality.

The pious Spaniard, Father Casasayas, was Tony's novice master. He taught Tony the art of prayer and meditation and awakened in him a deep taste for things spiritual. One of the important events during the noviciate was a thirty-day retreat, the famous *Spiritual Exercises* of Ignatius of Loyola. The young novice went through those 30 days in perfect silence, his day's programme being filled with meditations and spiritual exercises. The noviciate is also an initiation into the Jesuit way of life through the practice of poverty, chastity and perfect obedience. Much stress was laid on this last virtue. Ignatius wanted his men to be obedient *perinde ac cadaver* (just like a corpse) to the commanding authority, from major superiors to the least of the minor officials down to the beadle, one of the novices appointed by the novice master to carry his orders to the novices. To 'obey' like a corpse is not a real homage to the commanding superior, but the Jesuits understand what it means: obedience like in the army. Tony perfectly practised this virtue and lived it unconditionally throughout his life.

The Jesuit rules are, on the whole, healthy directives to aid men to develop moral and intellectual capacities for the service of the church. But, like in an army, (Ignatius was a soldier) the whole purpose of life is oriented to clear goals, so that whatever is emotional and belonging to the realm of feelings is quickly cut short. One of the rules embodying such an attitude is the 'rule of touch', whereby it is totally forbidden to touch another co-novice, give him an affectionate hug or show intimate brotherly affection by physical contact. Some novice masters went even further. Extending this rule of touch, they taught that it was forbidden even to fondle dogs or cats. A physical touch was tolerated only on extraordinary occasions, like when greeting a person at the profession of the first or the last vows. After pronouncing the vows the Jesuit came out of the chapel and was congratulated by his companions with a warm hug. The novices craved for that occasion when they could touch and feel a human being even for a moment. Stricter novice masters would sometimes intervene to replace the hug by a formal handshake.

As a further interpretation of this rule, all particular friendships too were a taboo. Any expression of deep friendship shown to one particular person was quickly reprimanded and suppressed. A Jesuit grew in this way as an efficient soldier, but like a corpse regarding his feelings. The so-called Rules of Modesty, which are applied and followed in detail, seemed to give that particular 'Jesuit look' to the members of the Society of Jesus: serious, withdrawn, intellectual faces with a feigned smile, somewhat artificial in feelings and emotions. Tony certainly had great difficulties with such a Jesuit outlook on life, for later when he was in charge of training the youngsters, he would try to promote particularly the feelings and healthy friendships which, as he said with a grin on his face, couldn't be other than particular.

Another domain in which the young Tony excelled during this time was the famous 'Eleventh Rule' of St Ignatius. The founder exhorts his men in it to learn to love humiliations and rejections and to consider oneself as worthless trash:

> ... they would wish to suffer reproaches, slanders and injuries, and to be treated and accounted as fools (without at the same time giving any occasion for it), because they desire to imitate and resemble in some sort their Creator and Lord Jesus Christ, and to be clothed with His garments and livery since he clothed Himself with the same for our greater spiritual good, and gave us an example, that in all things, as far as

> by the assistance of God's grace we can, we may seek to imitate and follow Him, seeing He is the true way that leads men to life.
> *(A Summary of the Constitutions)*

This rule plays an important part in a Jesuit's formation and life. Many strive to be like Jesus (their nick-name *Jesuita* comes from Latin *Jesu-ita*, 'like Jesus'). In the spirit of this rule, as he understood it with the zeal of a novice, Tony would opt for the service of washing the toilets and bathrooms of the noviciate, a service that is seen as horrendous in India – impure work delegated only to the outcasts. The desire for humiliations for the love of Christ went further: he enjoyed shocking his mother when she came to visit. He would appear before her in a cassock soiled by the dirt of the pigsty in which he chose to work at that time. It was not just a wicked trick to shock the mother. It was a sort of self-hate going to the extent of hating motherly affection and love. *Agere contra* (act against your liking) – a self-torture in all things – was to be a sign of sanctity then. The young Tony succeeded this way in putting an end to his mother's visits. Whenever she rang the bell at the parlour, the porter was informed to tell her that Tony was out. The affectionate mother would wait for her son for hours, only to be informed later that a visit was no longer possible and that she had better return home.

At the end of two years of noviciate, filled with experiments in spiritual life, Tony was formally introduced into the Jesuit order as a formal student, or scholastic as they are called, through the taking of the religious vows of poverty, chastity and obedience.

Thus began the long intellectual formation, the time during which the highest priority is given to studies and examinations. Spiritual life is not neglected but it is no longer in the forefront. The young Jesuit is now required to excel in intellectual pursuits. This intellectual formation starts with the so-called juniorate, normally done in the same house as the noviciate, and which also lasts for two years. In Tony's time, the young Jesuit, even in India, was intensely drilled in Latin, Greek and English. The later studies of philosophy and theology were done through the medium of Latin. English was then the Jesuit's working language. His companions recall how he went through these two years. The lanky and talkative youngster could speak and write fluent and elegant English and was even appointed as a 'tutor' for his fellow students requiring extra help. He was also at great ease with Latin and Greek. He was often found reading Homer in his spare time just as if he were reading a novel.

In those days, the Spanish Jesuits had a tradition of sending gifted Indian students to Spain for the following three-year training in scholastic philosophy. They believed that a better training would be given to the young Indians there and that it would create links with the mother province that sent missionaries to India. Naturally, the gifted Tony was chosen and sent to San Cugat, near Barcelona, where the Jesuits had a centre of studies. He spent three years there (1952-1955). It is difficult to say how much Tony was really interested in the drab scholastic philosophy that was taught there in Latin. He certainly did not neglect it, but his heart and mind were set already on spirituality. Evidently his first interest was in the Spanish mystics, Teresa of Avila and John of the Cross. He read their works in their original Spanish. He seemed to be fascinated with this language and his curiosity did not stop with the mystics. He read Cervantes in his spare time. I remember, some years later, he would encourage us to learn Spanish in order to feel the music of the mystical writings and to better understand the meaning behind the words of Ignatius of Loyola.

The contact with Father José J. Calveras, a great spiritual master and scholar in the *Spiritual Exercises*, was decisive for Anthony. Father Calveras used to take aside a small group of interested young Jesuits and initiate them in his own spiritual discoveries in the *Spiritual Exercises* of Saint Ignatius of Loyola. He felt that the contemporary Jesuits had unwittingly reduced these spiritual teachings to dry, almost intellectual feats. Their essence and purpose, according to Father Calveras, as Tony used to narrate to us, were feeling (*sentire*) and tasting (*sapere*) of spiritual savour deep in the senses. Tony's later *sadhana* ('meditating with mind and body') was probably born there. Back in India he would begin to experiment with spiritual techniques and methods used in the spiritual traditions of India and discover effective aids to help restore the *Spiritual Exercises* back to their original savour of feeling and tasting.

After these first five years of intense intellectual training, the young Jesuit scholastic is brought back from the secluded monastic life into contact with the real world, with men and particularly women who were, up until then, totally absent in the vicinity. That period of formation is termed 'regency'. The tender butterfly, which has just broken open the protecting cocoon, is exposed now to real situations in life. The young man is invited to make a deeper decision either to hold on to his choice of religious life or to give it up. Simultaneously, the superiors and seniors watch the young religious in his actions and reactions to the mundane situations of life. The regency is normally done in schools in the company of experienced Jesuits as well as lay teachers.

On his return to Bombay in 1955, Tony was assigned for his regency to St Mary's School at Byculla, in the heart of the city of Bombay. A year's stay there was enough to convince one and all that the young man was solidly rooted in his spiritual choice and pursuit. Furthermore, they needed his services at the noviciate and juniorate of Vinayalaya to teach English and possibly other languages. His students remember him as a joyful person, full of jokes and anecdotes, which brought life into an otherwise very quiet, drab atmosphere of a monastic house. There, he made his first attempts at writing and publishing. The booklets he wrote were humorous anecdotes about what happened within the walls of Jesuit houses. The unsaid purpose was clear: to give high school boys a taste, even fascination, for Jesuit spirituality. They did, in fact, inspire vocations. But senior Jesuits found them a little too unrealistic, picturing an all too happy-go-lucky idea of Jesuit life, which was not generally the case. And so their publication came to an early end.

The following stage in the formation is studies in theology for a period of four years. Normally, at the end of the third year, the young Jesuit, nearing now almost thirty years of age, is ordained a priest. From then on, although still in formation, he is given sufficient liberty to live an adult life, to express himself through a pastoral activity and act responsibly on his own, taking up imaginative initiatives in the religious and academic life. Tony did his theological training at De Nobili College in Pune (then known as Poona). The house is named after the renowned missionary Roberto de Nobili (1577-1656), a scholarly Jesuit who came to India from his native Rome to preach the gospel. Despite fierce opposition from his brethren and from other ecclesiastical authorities, he gave up the Jesuit cassock and put on the loin clothes of a learned Brahmin, in order to preach the gospel in an atmosphere which was familiar to the Hindus. With his head shaven, except for a small strand of hair, symbol of scholarship, he began to preach the Christian faith in Sanskrit and Tamil, and in the traditional Hindu categories and terms. This bold inculturation did create a Christian fold, but his opponents succeeded in inciting Rome to decree its death. Today, the theologate De Nobili College forms part of a vast campus, the Jnana Deepa Vidya Pith, with faculties of philosophy and theology, where over a thousand young men and women from all over India are trained for Christian ministries and education.

Tony spent four years (1958-1962) on this campus. As with all other studies, he excelled in theological learning, which was then a pre-Conciliar theology taught in Latin and where, in total contradiction of De Nobili's method, the young Indians were obliged to hear lectures in Latin and pass the oral examinations in Latin. But the campus was always known for its innovative initiatives in Christian pastoral and religious life. With Conciliar theologians like Josef Neuner amongst his professors, the openings towards Vatican II were beginning to be seen.

Although a brilliant student, Tony did not seem to have shown a particular interest in theology. The teaching staff, as well as the students of De Nobili College, were becoming more and more conscious of the need to give an Indian face to the church in India, which projected an all-too-Western image. Tony began to expose himself to Indian religions, particularly to Hindu pundits and intellectuals for which the city in which he lived then, Pune, is known in India. He read Hindu scriptures, visited Hindu shrines and ashrams, and had regular contacts with Hindu and Jain masters of spirituality.

At the end of his third year in theology, Tony was ordained priest on 23 March 1961 at St Peter's Church of his native Bandra, where he was baptised in 1931.

ANTHONY DE MELLO

Training in psychology

The last year of theology at De Nobili was already a preparation for what was to come later. His interest in the Ignatian *Spiritual Exercises* and spiritual counselling grew all this time, but he had already made his fundamental choice in life: to become a missionary. It was a decision taken long before, in the early years of the noviciate, a decision full of challenge that required a lot of self-sacrifice for which he was ever ready. However, in the last years his interest had grown particularly in the field of spirituality. He had to make a clear decision now. He opted for the study of spirituality only as an alternative, should his first choice – to become a missionary – be turned down by the superiors.

At that time, the need to integrate psychology and psychological counselling in spirituality and in spiritual guidance was keenly felt in all schools of spirituality and in all centres of spirituality. People everywhere felt that a genuine spirituality was possible only when it was backed by a healthy psychology. Father Edward Mann, an American, then provincial superior of the Jesuits in Bombay, suggested that Tony be trained to become a spiritual counsellor. He did not take into consideration Tony's missionary zeal but ordered him to take up further studies in psychology at the Department of Psychology at the Loyola University in Chicago. The obedient Tony had no choice. He left for America in 1963.

While working for the Master's degree in counselling, he attended lectures given by psychologists belonging to different schools of thought. We know from Tony's later talks that he was quite familiar with Transactional Analysis, Gestalt and other schools of psychology. His stay in America brought him the opportunity to come in contact with lay people and lay thinkers. Up till then he had been involved rather exclusively with religious people. Most of his masters in Chicago were lay people and so were the co-students. Tony had to confront more and more secular and non-Christian situations where he had to translate traditional Christian and Jesuit thought into a modern-world context. People with whom he moved about were not churchgoers, nor were they closely associated with church activities. They were free thinkers who sought meaning in their lives by experiencing spiritual elements from all religions. As an

Indian Jesuit, he had to react to the profound fascination that many Westerners showed to non-Christian religions of Indian origin, like Hinduism and Buddhism. This roused in him not only a deeper interest in the religious thought of his own country, but also a challenge to promote Christian spirituality in India by making use of the vast and deep spiritual heritage of Indian religious traditions.

It is probably at this point that he wrote the conferences which were published after his death in a book entitled *Contact with God* (1990). Many of these talks reflect his early spirituality in which the whole emphasis is on prayer and the need for prayer in daily life. Although he does not bring in elements from other religions, he opens up the Ignatian concept of prayer to other methods of prayer, particularly the Jesus Prayer and other forms known in Christianity, and shows the possibility of integrating them in the Christian spiritual experience.

Carl Rogers (1902-1987), whom Tony quoted frequently, was one of the psychologists from whom he learnt the concepts of acceptance, empathy and congruence. *Acceptance* is the continual attention paid to the other – to what the other is in reality and not the manner in which one would like to assume him to be. *Empathy* is the ability to feel what the other person feels and to communicate in depth with him. *Congruence* is the awareness of one's own feelings towards the other person and the readiness to make them known to the other. Eric Berne (1910-1970) was another psychologist whom he liked, particularly his 'Art of Awareness' that came very close to the art of attention, which is the basic approach in meditation. Tony also admired and recommended Fritz Perls (1893-1970), in particular his saying, 'Don't push the river'. Tony was certainly influenced by Barry Stevens (1902-1985) when he taught that 'Happiness is letting the happenings happen'.

What, in fact, Tony learnt from the psychologists in America was a therapy, an art of healing that could be applied to the spiritual domain. He appreciated very much Carl Rogers' non-directive counselling but did not follow it very closely for he was probably too impatient for such a method to act upon the clients. He wanted quicker results and so developed his own methods of bringing healing in life through what his religious master

Ignatius of Loyola had taught as the 'discernment of spirits'. Right discernment leads a person to the state of non-attachment or detachment, which is, according to Ignatius of Loyola and the Indian mystics, the true health-bringing state of life, an effective therapy for the many of man's maladies.

During his stay in America, Tony spent his weekends giving talks and retreats to a variety of people. He was in great demand in the Catholic as well as the secular centres. Invitations to give talks and reviews on television multiplied, and his popularity as a preacher spread far and wide in America. His stay there was primarily to acquire experience in psychology, which he gained abundantly, although he did not identify himself as belonging to any one of the then existing American schools of psychology. He assessed later that most of what he had heard in America in the centres for studies in psychology was absolutely a waste of time, whereas the contacts he had with earnest people in search of truth was indeed enriching to him. This acquired psychological training lasted for a long time in his spiritual development. As this training in America was planned as a first step towards his formation as a spiritual master, he left America in 1964 to begin formal training in spirituality in Rome.

But Rome apparently did not offer him what he was seeking nor contribute further to what his American experience had brought him to appreciate in spirituality and counselling. His stay there lasted only about a year. The study of spirituality conducted in an academic context in the Roman universities seemed to him to be unrealistic. He had already gained experience during his stay in Spain with masters of Spanish mysticism. His knowledge of Ignatian spirituality gained during the last years, coupled with his recently acquired psychological knowledge, were beginning to create a spiritual synthesis in him, to which Rome had then apparently little to contribute. He cut short his stay there and returned to India in 1965, and after pronouncing the Final Vows, which made him a professed and permanent Jesuit closing the long period of formation. It was time to start working in the world, with real life situations.

WHO IS ANTHONY DE MELLO?

Missionary life
Tony's desire to become a missionary, as we noted, had started very early in his life as a young Jesuit novice. In the Indian context, missionary life meant going out to forlorn villages and the undeveloped countryside to live there with the poor villagers and work for their development, together with the preaching of the good news of Jesus Christ. That way of life was in total contrast with that of the Jesuits working among the richer populations in the cities of India, in good schools and in comfortable houses. In his noviciate days Tony had heard from a superior on visit how Jesuits, after years of intellectual pursuits, lose fervour in their spiritual life and settle down to a comfortable routine. The test to prove that one's spiritual life was alive consisted, according to this superior, in the readiness to go to the mission stations and to live there as a missionary. This 'test' was somehow engraved in Tony's heart and mind as a challenge in life.

His offer to be a missionary was refused after his ordination. But now it came, almost fell on him, not from his own choice but ordered by the Provincial Superior who probably wanted to test the real sense of obedience of this young psychologist and popular and renowned preacher, freshly returning from the West. He bluntly told Tony that he needed a good missionary in the mission stations, and that he had the intention of sending him there. Tony, as he confessed to us later, resented this very much because the call was not, so to say, a brave and generous choice made from his own free will but a somewhat crude and unexpected move of a superior. Settled in the mission station of Shirpur (Central India), he would give vent to this resentment by trying to punish, so to say, his fellow Jesuits who opted for a pastoral life in the cities. He would constantly draw the attention of everyone to the need to send Indian missionaries to places which were occupied by the Spaniards and thereby try to drag into mission stations those who were settled in a comfortable life. He was giving us thereby an illustration of how guilt feelings, even in spiritual life, provoke the malicious desire of self-torture and the torture of others.

My first meeting with Father Anthony De Mello was at this time, that is in 1966, when I was a student at De Nobili College. Tony used to drop in from time to time at his *alma mater*, whenever business brought him over to the city from his forlorn Shirpur. He seemed fully engaged in missionary life with zeal, having a real try at inculturation, which was then a new subject of conversation among theologians and missionaries. One of the attempts to implement inculturation was trying to become more Indian. The missionaries used to a Western way of life were slowly trying to live like simple Indians. The Bombay-bred Goan, Anthony de Mello, was squatting on the floor, eating food with fingers from the *thali* (large metal plate) and, to show how deeply he had immersed himself into the village way of life of the Marathis, he would even belch, which was a sign of satisfaction in the Indian village.

However, he came to us at De Nobili, not so much to convince us of his missionary life, but as to satisfy our thirst for psychology applied to spiritual life. All of us had plans then to become spiritual psychologists. Contact with him began with an annual retreat of eight days. We noticed that he was a preacher unlike the others we were used to. He seemed to preach spirituality in a newer, fresher way, making it a joyful experience in comparison to our old spiritual fathers, whose counsels and exhortations were highly soporific. What he taught was not new. He would bring us back to what he termed fundamentals of spiritual life. For example he spoke with unction of mortification and of fasting as wonderful means of awakening the spirit from within. There was also a lot of applied psychology. He had begun to seriously apply Transactional Analysis and Gestalt to the problems of spiritual life. We formed for the first time 'workshops' on the subject of group therapies and group counselling. The pursuit of such a spirituality inspired much confidence and hope for the future. We formed around him a small team of young Jesuits interested in spirituality and in the application of psychological principles to spirituality, group dynamics and counselling. The first sadhana group was being birthed there.

Retreat Master and spiritual counsellor
Tony's missionary experience did not last very long. The superiors were convinced of the obedience of this gifted and highly popular Jesuit. They were in need of a dynamic and creative person to form the young Jesuits at the noviciate and juniorate Vinayalaya.

WHO IS ANTHONY DE MELLO?

When Tony took over the charge as rector there in 1968, things began to move quite visibly and very fast in an otherwise quiet and routine-bound Jesuit house. He began to reform things outright, but the reform began with himself.

His experiments were first tried in the laboratory of his personal life before applying them to others. He seemed to be at war against the way of life of the Jesuits in Bombay City and elsewhere. It did not reflect the ideals of poverty and asceticism of religious life for a country like India, rich with its own religious and spiritual traditions for millennia. He felt that what the Jesuits needed was the experience of stark poverty, intense prayer and the direct experience of God. The young Jesuits saw their rector abandoning his spacious room to live in a small crammed stockroom under the staircase. Poverty and living with a minimum of things was his way of life. He deemed that it was the most important condition to follow Jesus and to be *Jesuita*, like Jesus.

The young students of Vinayalaya, who were just beginning the Jesuit way of life, began to copy the example of the rector and started to live the ideal of poverty according to the expectations of the poor around in the city, by giving up comforts that were available in the house. They began to go about in the loin clothes of the Bombay poor, bringing into the clean Jesuit houses the 'unwashed', sick and homeless persons of Bombay city. This, of course, irritated the well-established elder Jesuits. But Tony was in support of the youngsters, defending their need to experiment with their own fantasies. This included sometimes the revival of some of the old Jesuit so called 'experiments' around the time of Ignatius of Loyola. Some tried living the life of a mendicant for a month, sustaining themselves solely on alms.

The second point on which Tony based the Jesuit renewal in life was prayer. He insisted on the fact that Ignatius and his companions prayed five hours a day – men of prayer who gladly spent hours of their precious time in prayer. The fundamental purpose of Ignatian spiritual exercises, according to him, was to bring men to the state of prayer, that is, the state of consolation, joyfully experiencing God's presence in all moments of the day. Prayer was to be a joyful experience in life and not a cumbersome activity. According to Tony, it was a grave mistake to regard moments of consolation as exceptions in spiritual life. They were meant to be the ordinary state of life of a man of prayer, of a Jesuit engaged in the service of the church. When he spoke of prayer, he radiated a certain force around him that often awakened in the heart of his hearers a real taste for prayer.

The simplicity of life acquired through intense poverty, and its spiritual depth sensed in prayer, was meant finally to lead to direct experience of God. Tony was convinced that the purpose of the Ignatian *Spiritual Exercises* was this direct encounter with God, an idea that he began to put forth in his prayer meetings and spiritual sessions. He even went on to say that such a direct experience of God was not the privilege of a few mystics, but that it was a natural right of every Christian. Similar teachings had already brought upon the founder of the Jesuits, Ignatius of Loyola, the suspicion of the Inquisition, who demanded from him in Paris more than a *Notification*. Ignatius was summoned to defend himself before the Inquisition from which he came out unscathed but with great difficulty. He was alive, and so could he defend himself against the church authorities of those days.

The long retreat movement began at this time, when Tony's efforts for a revival in prayer were yielding results with Jesuits and other religious people who came to hear him. The success of an eight-day retreat at a Jesuit house prompted him to propose a long retreat to a mixed group. Normally, Jesuits make a long retreat, which lasts for thirty days, twice in their life: at the beginning of their formation, that is, during the noviciate, and a second time at the end of their formation, which is called 'tertianship'. But Father Tony saw no point in limiting this experience to only twice in a lifetime and so he suggested that people do it whenever they felt the need for it. The success was great. Those who undertook it began to feel in their lives the power of prayer and meditation. So began a series of long retreats, which Father Anthony de Mello was preaching three to four times a year. He was invited all over India and the Far East, to countries like Singapore, Malaysia and Japan, where his retreats became very popular. These long retreats, under his guidance, were not just moments of intense prayer and silence but they had a healing effect on people, particularly on those who were in the process of making a life-changing decision.

The interest in the *Spiritual Exercises* that Father de Mello succeeded in creating in people lay not only in his spiritual and personal charisma but also in the art of counselling that he brought into the age-old Ignatian spirituality. He was up to date with the latest techniques, which he learnt in America and elsewhere. However, people flocked to him not only for this technical know-how. De Mello was, in fact, his own school of counselling, with his own methods, which sometimes were not at all in accord with the psychological theories of schools. He had the innate art of listening to people that made one feel that he was there exclusively for his client. Secondly, with his techniques and help, which we shall see more closely in the following chapters, he would make the *Spiritual Exercises* a living experience.

Tony's counselling was never abstract or theoretical. He brought his clients quickly to gain insight into life's problems. He counselled in private, but his preference was group therapy. However, at that time group dynamics was something new to religious people. Some of the participants were not ready to come out with their personal problems before a group, and it required some tact to make them speak. We will treat this part of Tony's pedagogical capacities in a later section on his art of spiritual guidance.

Discovery of Indian Masters
At this stage of his life, that is around 1970, after some years of intense spiritual activity on Indian soil among priests and nuns, but also a variety of other people with whom he met and talked, he became more and more interested in the methods and techniques of Oriental spiritual masters. It is difficult to say how much Tony studied other religions formally. But, being a voracious reader and studious experimenter, he had, in fact, visited many monasteries and contacted spiritual people of other religions. His knowledge of Buddhism seems to be very deep, which is evident from his stories and reflections. However, Tony never quoted, so to say, the teachings of other religions in support for his spiritual ideas, probably for two reasons. First, for him, a spiritual idea was not valuable because it was based on a spiritual authority but because it had a direct impact on the life of the person who assumed it. Second, quoting the scriptures of

different religions becomes often a futile exercise and a waste of time since scholars are rarely in agreement over their interpretations of the teachings. Tony avoided such discussions in his group counselling. All that he borrowed from other religions was somehow filtered through his own personal experience and invited a personal response from his listeners.

Some of these masters had, at that time, an immense renown and following in the West. In particular, Jiddu Krishnamurti (1895-1986) was very active both in the East and in the West. His books and his televised talks were highly popular everywhere. Even in a non-English speaking country like Switzerland, he attracted at Gstaad over 5,000 listeners every summer. Tony was very much taken up by his ideas, such as freedom in education, religion as being sensitive to reality, seeking God by abandoning the ideas we make of him and so forth. Life in its present reality meant, for Krishnamurti, a thought process; real life, however, was over and above it. Later on, Tony strongly recommended us to read one of Krishnamurti's books, *Think on These Things* (New York, Harper and Row, 1964; published also elsewhere under the title *This Matter of Culture*), warning us that it might change our life. I think that is what Tony looked for in all that he heard and read: things that change and transform life.

More modest, yet still powerful, were the Vipassana meditation techniques of S. N. Goenka. This Indian businessman, who picked up the ancient Buddhist method of meditation in Burma from another layman, U Ba Khin (1898-1971), had been teaching relentlessly to crowds of people, learned as well as simple uneducated people in India and in other countries. On account of its simplicity, the method of Vipassana is regarded as that which the Buddha himself practised. It consists of the awareness of breathing in and out and the sensations in the body. The practice of it, prolonged over a few days, can bring about enormous changes in life, for it acts like a powerful ploughing of life's field, unearthing deep hidden impurities and blockages in all levels of life. Father de Mello would recommend that the participants of sadhana try a session of Vipassana under this master.

In 1980 I also had the chance of doing a ten-day Vipassana under Goenka in Hoch Ybrig in Switzerland and, the following year, another session with an American pupil of U Ba Khin, John

Coleman. Both of these experiences opened my eyes to realities that my Christian and Jesuit education alone had not led me to realise. I have since then become a fervent practitioner of this meditation. Several meditations in Father de Mello's sadhana come from the Vipassana tradition. Tony had certainly tried Zen but had not been fond of it, perhaps because of its rigid atmosphere where talking (which is essential for Tony) was prohibited during the sessions.

The centre of the renowned but also notorious spiritual master, Rajneesh (1931-1990), known in the West by his title Bhagavan, meaning 'Blessed Lord' or, later, by Osho, meaning 'The Awakened', was just four kilometres away from De Nobili College in Pune where Father de Mello had settled in 1972 to begin his spiritual exercises and experiments of sadhana. De Mello had come to know this master even earlier through his numerous books, which he read with interest and with a certain admiration. However, Rajneesh was taboo not only for the Christians but also for the Hindus on account of his provocative teachings and what appeared in public as very liberal behaviour in sexual relationships. Many people in Pune were shocked by the Westerners who flocked to him. Upon arrival in the city, they donned the ochre robes reserved in the Indian religious traditions for the renunciates. But these were anything but renunciates, for they were often seen frequenting the best and most expensive restaurants, cafés and hotels of Pune (thereby provoking an unsupportable inflation for the local people). Indians were shocked to see couples in close physical contacts, sometimes seen making love in public under the trees and bushes of Rajneesh's gardens.

I do not know whether or not Tony went to Rajneesh's centre to listen to the master. But I did on some occasions, paying the rather heavy entrance fee for non-members. On one such occasion, Rajneesh was making a résumé of his teachings. He said man was like a tree. It grew healthy, high and wide if it had enough water, heat and air; otherwise, it would diminish and dry up. That was to be the model for human life: if one has enough of life's possibilities, that is health and wealth, then one can go for all pleasures that can be desired until one has the feeling of perfect satisfaction. One should have no feelings of guilt about that. There is no such thing as a prefixed notion of a good or bad character – a central theme in his teachings. Character is what one *is*, not what one acquires by modelling oneself on the norms set by others, or worse, by being a victim of modelling done by others in society. The Western and the rich Indian audience embraced this precept with great joy. But Rajneesh's second precept was not so easily practised: when you have nothing and when you are penniless, do not let yourself drown in sadness and depression. Learn to be happy there, too, even to die and disappear, for there is then nothing more for you to get out of this life.

I met Tony that day at the recreation-lounge after lunch. I told my fellow Jesuits there that I went to hear Rajneesh. Tony, who was browsing through the newspaper, suddenly got interested in my talk: 'What do you think of him?' he asked me. 'Well,' I said, 'he appears to cater to his audience.' Tony smiled and went on reading his newspaper. I think I read Tony's thoughts in that smile: 'Poor chap, you understood nothing.' Tony probably admired the basic soundness of Rajneesh's teachings. But he took him always very cautiously, for there were many who misunderstood him and deviated from the real sense of his teachings. Unlike the Christian masters, Rajneesh was an absolutely free thinker who aired out his views and positions to one and all with absolutely no feelings of responsibility towards any one. He left his hearers fully free to do what they desired. Fulfilment of desires as a first step was the central point of his teachings. He would not interfere in the personal life of his hearers in life nor in their death, even when there was danger of frustration, depression and suicide or murder. Father Anthony de Mello, on the contrary, also a renowned spiritual master in Pune, rather taught the rules of discernment, which had no place in Rajneesh teachings. Tony never spoke of Rajneesh in public nor did he encourage people to go to him. However, he recommended sometimes Rajneesh's, *The Book of the Secrets* (Rajneesh Foundation, Pune, 1974), which is a free commentary on an important Hindu-Buddhist Tantric meditation book, *vijnana-bhairava-tantra* or 'the art of shattering the knowledge'. This particular Buddhist work, a compendium of 112 meditations was probably one of de Mello's sources for his experiments in meditations.

Anthony de Mello must also have come to know Ajahn Chah (1917-1992) during his travels to the Far East. This renowned Thai Buddhist master, who spent the last six years of his life in a comatose state with absolutely no intake of food, had a large following in the West. His teachings are carried over today by some earnest Western monks who name themselves as belonging to the 'Forest Monastery Tradition'. Ajahn Chah's teaching was a permanent commentary on the Buddhist fundamental principles of *anicca* ('impermanence') and *anattha* ('soul-lessness'). He spoke in simple words of the transitory nature of all one holds on to, even one's most personal concepts and categories of thought. Becoming fully aware of this nature of mind and being was to be the soul of spirituality. A strong influence by this school of thought can also be seen in de Mello's teachings but brought into connection with the Christian impermanence of life and the permanence of the kingdom of God. Anthony de Mello spoke of this master and his own desire to live and teach like him in the last letter he wrote to a friend, just moments before his death:

... The things that mattered so much in the past do not seem to matter any more. Things like those of Ajahn Chah, the Buddhist teacher, seem to absorb my whole interest and I am losing my taste for other things.

(quoted by Parmananda Divarkar S.J., *Prayer of the Frog* I, xviii)

What exactly was Tony looking for in these masters? In the first place, his interest was not directly in Hinduism, Buddhism or any other religion. He was exclusively interested in spirituality and spiritual experience and had an immense curiosity to experiment with spiritual techniques. However, his growth was profoundly in his own Christian roots. He writes in the introduction to *The Song of the Bird*:

I have wandered freely in mystical traditions that are non-Christian and even non-religious and they have profoundly influenced me. It is to my church, however, that I keep returning, for she is my spiritual home; and while I am acutely, sometimes embarrassingly, aware of her limitations and her occasional narrowness, I am also aware of the fact that it is she who has formed and moulded me and made me what I am today.

In all his experiments with spiritualities he nourished and cherished this unconditional love and affection for the church, and this until his death.

I think his interest in spiritualities took him only where he could try, on his own, a given spiritual experience and experiment with it. He showed little interest in a mere spiritual teaching, however interesting it might be. That explains perhaps his choice of Oriental teachers and traditions. He did not show a particular interest in masters like Tagore, Ramana Maharshi, Nityabodhananda, Ananda Moyi and those others who are numerous on the Hindu religious scene. A voracious reader of all sorts of books, he picked and chose those that gave him a chance to experiment.

In this context, I remember his meeting with Swami Abhishiktananda (1910-1973), the French Benedictine monk Dom Henri Le Saux who lived as a Hindu sage in the Himalayas. As a young Jesuit, I was fascinated by his teachings and his way of life that was dedicated to the contemplation of the Mystery of the Holy Trinity in expressions and symbols of the ancient Hindu Upanishads. I remember my first visit to him in the summer of 1968. While young people of my age in Europe were then in revolution, I was spending quiet moments of meditation in the small hut of Swami Abhishiktananda on the banks of the rapid Ganges at Uttarakashi, high up in the Himalayas. A few months later, Father de Mello, then rector of Vinayalaya, invited Le Saux to his noviciate in the company of Sisters Sara Grant and Vandana, who were also admirers and ardent followers of Swamiji in their efforts at inculturation in Bombay. It was a meeting that these pioneers in inculturation were organising for the benefit of their young men and women in training. The centre of the discussion was contemplation and liturgy. Swami Abhishiktananda celebrated his Sanskrit Mass for us all, seated on the ground as the Brahmin priests do. There was a lot of enthusiasm for it among the young religious men and women.

We met again a few months later at Bangalore for the All India Seminar. Father de Mello also attended it as a delegate from Bombay. However, his participation was not particularly noteworthy for he seemed rather bored by the abstract theological discussions that were taking place there. But he spent long time in conversation with Swamiji. Both had a spiritual vision for the future of India, but the church in India was not quite ready to pay attention to them.

Abhishiktananda was also full of sympathy for Father de Mello's spiritual ideas and approach. But psychology and counselling were not his 'daily bread'. De Mello on his part did not seem too keen on the experiment of Henri Le Saux. He was very appreciative of it, but the experiment appeared to him to be too sanskritised and traditional, abstract and not sufficiently rooted in real life. Le Saux had apparently no key to spiritual experience, although he spoke about it at length by bringing his Western monastic experience to the Hindu spiritual teachings and traditions. In Tony's opinion, the religious in India and particularly the Jesuits, had had enough of tradition; what they needed was experience. Here one can notice de Mello's real attitude towards the Eastern religions and wisdom. De Mello in fact did not go in for inculturation as such. He did not really care for traditions or cultures; nationalities, national heritage and the like was not what he sought. Men and women, as human beings, independently and in spite of all their cultural differences, were his main interest.

Anthony de Mello's interest in the Oriental masters was partly awakened by his Western audience, first in America and later on in India. People in the West were apparently deeply interested in Eastern religions. It is their quest that prodded Tony to take a deeper interest in the Oriental spiritual experiences and elicit a reaction from the expert that he was in the *Spiritual Exercises*. In his Indian context too, he felt the need to integrate into his spiritual teachings ideas and practices from other religions in which neither he nor the church in India had until then showed a real interest. Secondly, it was becoming impossible to remain comfortably closed within the secure Western walls of Christianity in an India where other religions, notably Hinduism, were affirming themselves loudly and clearly. Until that time, the church in India had a feeling of superiority coupled with the colonial might. I remember how we were taught there in the catechism to shun all Hindu temples or gestures of worship. I came to know of the great Hindu spiritual masters like Ramdas and Muktananda, who were around my home town of Mangalore, only when I left India and was a student in Paris. The church teachers in those days in India never taught us to appreciate and honour the Hindu teachers. Anthony de Mello, who met, heard and read these masters, felt soon that spirituality in India was no longer credible if it did not have a relationship with the age-old spiritual traditions that had carried humanity through the ages.

Institute for Pastoral Counselling and Spirituality
In 1972, a new Provincial Superior had to be named for the Bombay Jesuit Province. Father de Mello was the choice of the majority of the Jesuits who had high hopes in him for the realisation of the new goals set for the post-Vatican II period. But Tony was not into it, not because he shunned the honour nor the service attached to this position, but he came to the conclusion through a rigorous spiritual discernment that his services were needed elsewhere more than in the provincial's office. In the spirit of the Jesuit motto, *Ad majorem Dei gloriam* ('for the greater glory of God'), he made known his choice to continue the spiritual renewal work that he had begun. It was clear to him that people needed him for spiritual training and pastoral counselling, which he could offer to a vast number of Jesuits and other religious in India and elsewhere.

De Nobili College in Pune offered him room to set up the Institute for Pastoral Counselling and Spirituality. He began to organise sessions there for Jesuits from all over India. He took the term *sadhana* to describe his method of counselling and spirituality for several reasons. In the first place, an Indian product needed an Indian name. *Sadhana,* a Sanskrit word that literally means 'Effort towards a goal,' is a very common term in Hinduism and Buddhism, especially in the spiritual context where it signifies an effort made to achieve a spiritual end. It stands for roughly what one calls 'spirituality'. There are, in fact, several different sadhanas in Hinduism and Buddhism but a renowned form of sadhana comes from what is known as 'Tantra', where the spiritual effort leading to the goal of liberation takes concrete forms of spiritual exercises, meditations, contemplation and therapies. I think Tony was influenced by this Hindu-Buddhist approach which employed techniques for spiritual experience much in the sense of Ignatius of Loyola's *Spiritual Exercises*.

With sadhana, he had given up giving the formal *Spiritual Exercises*, which he till then had so ardently and intensively taught to different groups. In 1976, when I came back to Pune after spending four years in Paris to obtain two doctorates, I felt an intense need to refresh my spiritual life. Intellectual pursuits coupled with mundane Parisian life had left me in a somewhat unbalanced spiritual state. Father de Mello had already set up his sadhana sessions at the De Nobili College. I asked him if I might do the *Spiritual Exercises* under his guidance. 'No,' came the answer. 'I have given up giving the *Exercises*. You see, Anand, the problem with the Jesuits is that the *Exercises* do change their life. But only for three months. Then they go back into their old rut. I have now created sadhana. It is very effective and will change you to the depths of your being, making you a new man.' He then offered me chance to join a sadhana, which would start the following week. I gladly took it up and went through an intensive work with him for three weeks. He was right – it changed my whole outlook in life. I began to see that I did not have a religious, Jesuit vocation. I was merely holding on to it as an ideal in life, but I was not really called to live a life of poverty, chastity and obedience as the Jesuits understood it. I felt God was calling me to something else – a more simple and joyous life with and in the world, above all, a life of liberty and freedom. This discovery filled my heart with a gush of joy. Within a few days, I decided to leave the Company of Jesuits without regret or pain. I have, however, not left them in my heart. I was and still am perfectly thankful to Tony.

Anthony de Mello's first book, *Sadhana – A Way to God*, appeared in 1978. The book marks the essential spiritual growth in his life, particularly through the spiritual experimentation he undertook in the previous ten years ever since he began his active pastoral work in India. Tony was not a writer. Whenever he had to write something (except personal letters, of which he wrote thousands) for publication, he would take extraordinary pains to read and re-read the manuscripts. But he was never satisfied with what he wrote, because his ideas would evolve so fast that the written sentence would appear sterile. However, *Sadhana – A Way to God* came into being because of the persistence of a friend of his, a nun (who wants to keep her anonymity), who persuaded him to produce a book for which people all over the world were waiting. She persuaded him by offering him suitable lodging in her convent, took care of his food and health and, above all, offered him what he did not have: time to write. Tony remained locked in this convent for three weeks, cut out from all phone calls and visits. That is how the first book came to fruition. But, again, just as it came out, Tony already felt estranged towards it. People were 'worshipping' the book and were practising the meditations by following the instructions too literally. Tony found this a little stifling because he felt himself bound to the written word and to a fixed and limited space of a book. One of his friends notes:

> The book *Sadhana – A Way to God* had just been released. With a twinkle in his eyes Tony shared with me how he visualised people buying the book, wanting to know what the sadhana course was all about, and being disappointed. 'Do they think we are doing prayer exercises all the time?' he quipped.
>
> No, sadhana as I experienced it is not doing prayer exercises all the time: it is a way of looking at reality 'prayerfully'. As one of my companions put it, 'Sadhana deals with God, spiritual problems, growth and people in the context of daily life.'
>
> (*We Heard the Bird Sing*, 52)

The uneasiness about this book remained in him till the end:
> Tony once told me personally: 'If I had to do it over again, I would not have written the book *Sadhana*.' That would have been a matter of weeks before he died. His most translated book, and he regretted having written it. I'm not sure why.
> (*We Heard the Bird Sing*, 110)

However, the book itself was tremendously successful. With it, Tony's popularity greatly increased all over the world, in all spiritual milieus. Today, the book has been translated into about

WHO IS ANTHONY DE MELLO?

fifty languages and has become a spiritual classic. In them, he brings his synthesis of spirituality to Christian spiritual life, an Ignatian spirituality of the *Spiritual Exercises* and modern psychological insights combined with Eastern spiritual methods of meditation and contemplation. Many have ever since experienced the powerful force those spiritual exercises have for piercing through the hard and rigid dross that surrounds the heart and for gushing out its fragrance of peace, contentment, joy, love and happiness, making prayer a delicious experience instead of a time of torture.

That was, in fact, his initial purpose in developing sadhana, which he meant to be an easy and delightful method of prayer for his Jesuit students and companions who found prayer 'dull and frustrating' (*Sadhana – A Way to God*, 3). He had previously brought out his prayer methods in cyclostyled pages, which were circulated among different people who tried them and found them very effective. One of his first experimental guinea-pigs was the Jesuit delegates to the General Congregation which met in Rome from December 1974 to March 1975. Every morning, Father de Mello, delegate of the Bombay Province, invited the members of the Congregation to pray according to his new sadhana methods. Apparently, the Congregation Fathers found them interesting and effective and made no negative judgements against them.

He brings together in this work, as St Ignatius did with his *Spiritual Exercises*, a variety of prayer methods. These methods include mental as well as vocal prayer, not excluding the petitionary prayer, whose purpose was to bring men into the presence of God and, therefore, into the presence of Love, Joy and Peace. He gives great importance to vocal prayer and to the prayer which goes by the name of the 'Jesus Prayer', an invocatory prayer linked to the rhythm of breathing. He saw there many similarities with the Hindu prayer of mantra-repetition. I think this initial interest in prayer of the Oriental church lead Tony more and more into experiments with methods of prayer of oriental religions, particularly in the field of meditation. It was technically at its perfection in the Hindu school of yoga and in the Buddhist eight-fold path leading man from his environment and from his individuality into the depth of his being, to the state where the mystic was in intimate union with the Being he or she sought.

Father de Mello has left a number of writings in the field of spirituality that have not yet been published. These are his spiritual notes and retreats, of which only a part was published in 1990 under the title *Contact with God*. He had the intention of working on these writings and publishing them one day. When one goes through some of these unpublished writings, one can notice his future growth in spirituality and the flowering forth of the spiritual experience into the state of liberty already present in seminal form in the early writings. The spiritual growth is evident, but the mystical heights did not belittle the prayer of the community, the ritual of those for whom it was essential. One can, therefore, say with certainty that at no moment did he give up prayer, the observance of his vows or the sacraments. He not only respected them but also lived by them intensely until the end of his life.

However, his spiritual vision had evidently changed. His way of looking at prayer, sacraments and all communitarian forms of Christian life and worship was now from a different angle. This new approach does not mean that he was estranged from them or that he denied them. He had simply evolved. The experienced mystic does not laugh at his earlier zealous days of novice-ship when, as a beginner, he was dependent on rules and methods. The highest pinnacle of mysticism reposes always on the first and lowest foundation.

However, his growth and his new approach to prayer and other forms of spirituality were remarked by people with a certain surprise. One of his students remembers the following:

Tony said to me: 'I gave myself fully to preaching retreats. Then I saw that 95% of religious are not ready for the retreats, hindered as they are by psychological problems. So I started sadhana and now I am fully in that period.' Then with a sparkle in his eyes he added: 'What will be next? I don't know. Maybe I'll marry ...'
(*We Heard the Bird Sing*, 110)

It was clear from the beginning that the Institute for Pastoral Counselling and Spirituality was to be only temporarily housed at De Nobili College. The presence of the so-called 'Sadhanites', and particularly the presence of women, seemed to disturb the smoothly-run religious house reserved exclusively for young men engaged in philosophical and theological studies. In addition, that atmosphere was not adapted to the Sadhanites, who too were living their experimental liberation and freedom in their spiritual experiments. Father de Mello gave serious thought to moving out. An old colonial-style building, the Stanislaus Villa, situated at Lonavla (forty kilometres away from Pune in the direction of Bombay) was offered to him to house his work. Having collected sufficient funds from friends and benefactors, Father de Mello had the old building renovated and a new one built there within a short time. The Institute of Pastoral Counselling and Spirituality, now renamed Sadhana Institute moved there in 1978.

Sadhana Institute
In Lonavla begins Father Anthony de Mello's last and final decade in life. The years spent there were probably the most important in his life, marked with rich spiritual experiments and discoveries. His life's model was changing from one determined by rules and regulations, traditions and structures to one of freedom opened up to the guiding Spirit in all situations and conditions of life. The particular Christian and Jesuit spirituality was widening to universal dimensions of a spirituality in which not only Christians but all people of good will from all religions and cultures felt at home. A good Christian spirituality, Father de Mello loved to repeat, should be good to all.

The house began to receive groups of religious men and women who came there for practical courses named sadhanas, under the guidance of Father de Mello and his assistants, Father Joe Aizpun and Father Dick McHugh. As in Pune, here also the offer was under the forms of maxi-sadhana, which lasted for about 9 months, and mini-sadhana whose duration was for 3 weeks. Apart from these regular courses, Tony sometimes offered the so-called 'renewal sadhanas' for those who were already familiar with the approach and who desired to re-kindle in their hearts the spiritual fire.

The daily programme of a sadhana was simple. The participants were free to rise at a time convenient to each in order to fulfil one's personal and spiritual obligations. Breakfast was served between 7:00 am and 8.30. The first session of the sadhana began at 9 am, often with one of Tony's assistants, who introduced a meditation or two and spoke about some fundamental teachings on the sadhana approach, inviting discussion over it as in a problem-centred therapy. Tony took over the group after the coffee break around 11 am. He rarely gave the meditations that he proposed in his books. Very often, he invited a question and went on and on analysing it till the lunch break at 12.30 and even sometimes in the afternoon, whenever there was a sadhana session scheduled. People were often dead tired listening to the non-stop flow of Tony's talks but at no moment given to boredom. For most, every instant seemed enthralling. Tony, however, apparently seemed always 'fit and trim' for more talk. Lunch was followed by a few minutes of sitting together over a cup of coffee and then everyone retired for a good siesta, which is 'a must' in India.

The participants in the sadhana often came with a heavy and accumulated charge of fatigue that needed to be blown off before they could intake the spiritual renewal. The afternoon was devoted to personal meetings with Father de Mello or with his assistants, for strolls or other forms of physical relaxation. Tony loved walks. He went alone for an evening walk in the natural green of Lonavla, sometimes accompanied by one of his numerous friends or by a person who asked for a personal talk with him. In the evening, the group met together for the concelebrated Mass. Tony loved to be the main celebrant. Strangely enough, in groups, he did not like to take a second place or be in situations in which he was not in the limelight. He gave a small homily after the gospel reading. With him as the celebrant, the Mass was invariably a homely, lively event of the day. After supper, the group sat together again with Tony cracking more wild jokes, laughing or watching videotaped programmes connected with sadhana. Tony gladly accepted invitations to dine outside in a restaurant or watch a film in the cinema whenever a good opportunity presented itself.

The sadhana in practice in Lonavla was quite different from that which he had written in his book, *Sadhana – A Way to God*. It certainly was *A Way to God* but not so directly as the book describes. Spirituality, in fact, meant at that time for him, not a series of 'exercises' but a continuous prayerful attitude in all that one did and experienced in life. He focused heavily on therapy and particularly on group therapy, more than he focused on meditation or contemplation. Although he gave much of his time to individual and personal spiritual guidance, he preferred group therapy, where the individuals exposed their problem to all in the group. In doing so, hidden aspects of problems experienced by different people were often brought out. Even though their lives were very different, many could thereby profit from the therapy suggested to one person in the group.

Role-playing was one of his preferred tactics for bringing people out of their cocoons. He would start by playing a role of a person with a problem. It looked imaginative and somewhat artificial but, in reality, it was a real problem of someone participating in the group that he had come to know outside of the group encounter. Playing the role of the client, he would seek counsel from the group, addressing a particular person. When that person had finished giving his counsel, he would request another person to continue counselling. This would help people to lose their shyness and more easily open up to sharing their own personal problems.

For example, a role-playing exercise would proceed as follows: Tony would start by saying, 'My name is Wilfred. I am a young priest of 35 years and I come to you, Dorothy (turning to one of the participants), for help. My problem is that I am appointed parish priest and, at the same time, I have to look after the management of a school besides being in charge of the estates. All this amounts to a terrible workload, which I assume, however, very well. I like the job, but there are moments where I am completely fatigued. Young women come to me for help, seeking counsel, and I like to help them in their life's problems. But there are moments when this help goes a little too far, and I start touching them, embracing them, kissing them and just feel their nearness, which, apparently, they don't dislike. It happens rarely that we spend the night together, and I must admit that sometimes I have gone too far by having sex with some of them. My problem is that I don't feel any conflict. I notice that this rela-

tionship brings relaxation to me and to the woman in question. We are happy for that. But once back in my room and to my normal work, I am filled with guilt towards my priesthood, towards my vow of chastity and towards the public who respect me. I have tried sometimes to stop all this, but it does not last very long. I fall victim to the same situations over and over again.'
Such role playing not only rouses the attention of the participants, but each participant begins to link the problem to his own personal problems, which slowly start coming up one after another, and the counselling takes place on the spot in common. Tony would then point out that which was good counselling and that where the counsellor should have limited the projection of his own problems in the situation. The counselling was never a condemnation of the person who narrated the problem. On the contrary, he was made to feel that all understood him and helped him to come to see it better, realise its causes and come out of it.

One important aspect of Father de Mello's sadhana was his humour. There wasn't a period of talk over ten minutes without a joke cracked and outbursts of hearty laughter following. His friends introduce the book, *We Heard the Bird Sing*, with a comment on his sense of humour:

> We missed Tony's jokes in the write-ups sent to us for the book. What is Tony de Mello without jokes? A man who, in the words of one of our writers, was 'a revered retreat-master and became the irreverent-director-of-sadhana', and who, in his own words, wanted 'to die cracking a joke'! And so we have thrown in a few – they are not his, but taken from other sources. We hope they have something of the two-edged humour and the wisdom-thrust of Tony's typical jokes.
> (*We Heard the Bird Sing*, Presentation)

If Father de Mello showed boundless love and compassion to those who came to him for help, this same love and compassion did not hinder him from applying harsh and painful shock therapies in groups. It was evident, although not always, to the client undergoing the therapy, that it was motivated by love and concern. These therapies consisted in suddenly and violently knocking off the protective armour that the person had built around himself through sheaths of psychic and spiritual elements of behaviour. Here is a typical case recounted by one of his sadhana clients:

> It happened in a session of maxi-sadhana. One day reluctantly I presented a personal problem to the group. Everyone bombarded me. As a finale Tony exploded dynamite, shattering all my defences. After the ordeal I couldn't eat or drink and I threw up repeatedly. I felt exhausted and lonely.
>
> Tony had given strict orders to the group not to meet me at all. However, a good Samaritan came to console me. Tony chased him away. The following day Tony said in the group that he loved me and knew that I had the resources to face the agony of growth. The painful silence was an experience of realising my own irrational views and of gaining growth-promoting wisdom.
>
> With cruel compassion, Tony had in a masterly fashion administered therapy to heal me. It was a turning point in my life.
>
> I was taking therapy from Tony in the group. Gradually I sank into a depression of sorts. One day, two days, several days – I continued in the depression. And I began to feel very angry with Tony. Why doesn't he help me out? More indirectly than directly I communicated this anger to him. All he said was: 'I love you much. It pains me to see you like this. You have a lot of strength within you.' I had learned something very valuable.
>
> (*We Heard the Bird Sing*, 36-37)

In one of the sadhanas I did under him, I experienced that Tony was trying shock therapy with me, too. I had just returned to Pune from Paris after a stay there for four years. I went to Tony to speak to him of my spiritual confusion, and he felt that I was a little too cerebral in my life. Furthermore, I had let my emotions and sentiments dry up, and I needed to get in touch with them. From that moment on, he would not give me an appointment. After days of waiting and repeated demands, he would give one only to cancel it at the last minute through a small note fixed on my door. Whenever I chanced to pass by him on the corridor or in the garden, he would physically run away from me. I guess he wanted to show the sort of emotional disgust he felt, which he wanted to communicate to me. Sometimes I used to barge in on conversations he made with others during the common recreations. He would cut short my remarks saying, 'Look, let us continue to speak a little more on the subject we're discussing right now.' Well, his therapy did not really have an effect on me. It did not make me break into sighs and sobs of emotions. In fact, the day I decided to change my way of life in quitting the Jesuit Order, he came to me to say: 'You know, Anand, I have all the time for you; you are free to come in to my room any time, all 24 hours.' I was, in fact, not fully at the end of the healing I was undergoing. My feelings still hurt, I just replied: 'Bye-bye, Tony.'

But the case of Father Thomas was different. He was fifty-five and a retired school teacher; a man who always smiled and wanted to joke in all conversations at all moments. One had the impression that one couldn't engage in a serious conversation with him. Once in the sadhana, he began to narrate to us how his life had been a success through God's blessings. Tony took up the dialogue with him and made him see that he was just putting on a happy face before others but that he had a lot of pain inside to hide. Tony then began to tear down his nervous and somewhat self-defensive mannerisms. At one point, Thomas broke down in tears and sighs, repeating continuously that his life was a failure and that he saw no reason to live any longer. The sadhana session ended rather sadly, each one retiring in silence. Apparently thereafter, Thomas engaged in several longer dialogues with Tony in private. But he was never again the same man. Laughter on his face had disappeared. On the last day of the sadhana, Tony spoke to us of the need to 'entertain always good feelings'. He asked us if we went away with good feelings. I reacted, saying that his treatment of Thomas was particularly one that did not produce 'good feelings', neither in Thomas nor in us. To which, of course, Thomas quickly objected saying that he was going away with very good feelings. Tony then took up: 'Anand, you will realise it one day. I know, you are not going away with good feelings; but you will realise one day the help I have given you.' True, he was perfectly right there. I realise it now, how every gesture and word was a help to get me out of my protective shell. However, Thomas died the year after. I wonder if the sadhana had something to do with it.

Most of the sadhana sessions were peaceful; rarely did the work become tumultuous and violent. However, on one occasion, some of us came to blows on a problem. Father Blaise was going blind. He was weak and fragile and spoke a lot about his steadily-weakening eyesight during the last years. Apparently, medical analyses and treatment brought no improvement. As Blaise was recounting his misfortune to us one day in the sadhana, Father Conrad, a stalwart missionary Jesuit from Northern India, sprang up and rushed at Blaise, caught hold of him by his neck, raised him up and began to shake him up like a plum tree, yelling, 'Speak the truth, stop pretending!' I could not bear this scene. I do not know what made me spring up to my toes and catch hold of Conrad, whom I, with all my strength, pushed down to the floor. People remarked that I was yelling profanities at him in French, his mother-tongue. All of this happened in a fraction of a minute. Others were watching the violent scene with consternation. Tony was quiet. When calm set in, Tony said: 'Do you realise, Anand, what a dangerous thing you did? Conrad could have killed you.' 'I am not a tender lamb to be killed so easily,' I retorted, 'and what were you doing then? You sat there sheepishly.' 'No, I was in possession of my feelings,' was Tony's calm reply, 'I was in fact waiting to see things happen.' 'I could not bear to see an innocent being attacked,' I was defending myself. The story came to an abrupt end there. Blaise, however, was not healed; and Conrad and I laughed over our anger and violence. We did not come back to that incident again in that sadhana, although some thought that I hindered Conrad's shock therapy that would have probably brought eyesight to Blaise.

Friends and Detractors

Much of the sadhana work, in reality, was a certain undoing of the so-called strict and rigorous religious formation that people underwent. Clerics and nuns – who were the exclusive participants in Father Anthony de Mello's sadhanas – were often moulded into unnatural forms of behaviour, or they themselves picked up unhealthy attitudes towards life, all in the name of the holy rules or with a misconceived 'supernatural' motivation. We have already remarked above how many Jesuits, from their early noviciate days, were warned against 'particular friendships', that is, the warm and tender feelings that one person could have for another in the community. This was seen as a disturbing factor in the community and contrary to the religious vow of chastity. Father de Mello, however, encouraged warm friendships. The problems of the religious were mostly in the domains of their vows, particularly what concerned chastity and obedience. A person recalls:

> In North India there is the feast of Raksha Bandhan. A girl ties a *rakhee*, an amulet of flowers or of ornamental paper or silver string, on the wrist of her brother or a male friend. The meaning is that the girl requests the man's brotherly care and protection over her, and he agrees. On Raksha Bandhan Day during the year of my sadhana, a woman in the group had a *rakhee* for each of the ten men in the group. I brought two *rakhees* to the group. I tied one on Tony's wrist and the other on the wrist of a friend. Tony burst out laughing and said: 'It is easy to tie a *rakhee* on everyone – none is left out; but it is difficult to choose one or two from the group, is it not?'
> (*We Heard the Bird Sing*, 12)

The fact was that many Jesuits cultivated such a universal outlook on friendship that they were lacking real emotional contact in human relationships with individuals. Tony, however, seemed to live particular friendships in his personal life. That was probably also one of the experiments applied to his person, to combat the deeply ingrained malformation towards friendship in the Jesuit way of life:

> One day Tony called me. Very honestly he told me he was feeling threatened and jealous because I seemed to be walking on air ever since a good friend of mine had arrived a few days earlier. I laughed aloud. 'Shanti, I am serious,' he said, 'I am feeling jealous and I am suffering and I am a neurotic.'
> (*We Heard the Bird Sing*, 24)

That was probably not a joke nor a subtle therapy. I think he needed deep friendship. One of his young confidants told me one day how Tony came to him one day with an urgent request: that he went to a convent some kilometres away from De Nobili College to tell Sister Catherine that Tony thought of her with love. That was probably a sequel to a therapy session. This Sister Catherine was known for her worldliness and snobbery which Tony had once attacked in a sadhana. She had broken down in sobs and tears. Was it a sweet consolation dispatched to her?

However, one of the subtle traps to which spiritual masters often fall victim is that they become slowly accustomed to a certain type of life in which they have to have something to do, where they ought to be in the limelight. Or else they do not come into the picture. A spiritual master, having become a master, loses the simplicity in life to learn things with others by becoming one among others. I wonder if Tony was not sometimes victim to this tendency. He certainly had a wonderful charisma to enliven conversations, group discussions and group therapies. Evidently, nobody else could do as well as he did. But one also felt that he had the need to be the centre of attention. One did not see Tony working with others or making himself one amongst others, or trying to find solutions in discussion with others. He was invariably the master in all situations. He seemed experimenting not just for himself, but mainly for others. And strangely he did not easily join in the experiments of others. Was this a conscious choice or a logical consequence to a habituated mode of life? In the field of spirituality, Anthony de Mello had much in common with another of his renowned countrymen: Mahatma Gandhi, the lonely but in the lone centre, living and working for others.

It would be unrealistic to think that he did not have detractors and enemies in life. It is natural that, in emotional experiments, one cannot avoid resentments. Some suddenly left the sadhana, pained or annoyed by Tony's treatment or analysis. Some others felt left out in his personal choice of friendships. Some others felt that they were not sufficiently recognised or appreciated by the master. One of such followers notes:

> I appreciated Tony greatly as I considered him an extraordinary person. When I try to recall my encounters with him, I am surprised to know that they were mostly negative. I did not like the way he avoided disagreement and confrontation by countering with an 'ad hominem' retort or attack. I was the victim of this repeatedly. Such experiences hurt me and confused me about him and distanced me somewhat from him emotionally. (*We Heard the Bird Sing*, 110)

But his real enemies, at least at that time, were not from among those who heard him and let themselves be guided by him. The real detractors of Father de Mello were those who did not come in direct contact with him but remained in the shadows of idle talk and gossip, prejudices and misinterpretations that were coined against his teachings and ideas. These were mostly from among his own Jesuit brethren. Some of them, engaged in social work, for example, felt that his spirituality was a self-centred spirituality that sought one's own moments of happiness and joy instead of concentrating on the social problems. They missed the point of what Tony said about attachment and the programming of the mind. Those again who lived the Jesuit rule in fear and awe, felt he was going too far. They would look for spiritual and theological arguments to put up barriers. There were some who could not stand Tony's talkative nature mixed with jokes and boisterous laughter. A few serious theologians, who never heard him or read him seriously, thought he was supplanting the Jesuit spirituality with a Hindu-Buddhist spirituality. In my opinion, these enemies and others have been behind the Roman *Notification*, which will be presently studied in this book.

The life of a detached person can sometimes be shocking to those who live under the burden of attachment, including attachment to rules and regulations. Father de Mello was once taken to task by some fellow Jesuits who had apprehensions about his spiritual guidance in fields of morality, especially in sexuality. A commission was set up to study this matter. The members of this commission, who were outside the sadhana circles, went about a thorough investigation by consulting all those who took part in Tony's sadhanas until then. That was around the time when some young Jesuits in America and elsewhere had brought forth a concept called the Third Way. They said that between a life of sexual commitment and sexual renunciation there could be a third way where spirituality could be lived with sexual relationships. When the matter went a little too far, the then general of the Jesuits, Father Arrupe, wrote a strong letter declaring this third way, where a Jesuit can sink in the arms of a woman in a closed car, was incompatible with religious life.

The apprehensions against de Mello rose from the fact that

sadhana sometimes created moments of euphoric joy, expressed through hugs and expressions full of emotions; situations where, if the person is not solidly grounded in detachment, he can often be a victim of new attachments, particularly in sexual matters. If these intense moments are lived like an exposure to a passing cool breeze, there is no danger. But when the need for physical contact becomes a daily and invincible need, then one has already fallen victim to one's attachment. When participants of sadhana brought up this matter for discussion, Tony did not quickly brush it aside. He did not advise, as the serious, traditional spiritual Fathers would have done, to run away from the physical temptation of sex. He counselled people to watch and be aware where it led them, discerning the attachment behind it. He was not promoting thereby easy physical and sexual relationships. Tony argued that, by giving vent to physical relationships early on, the development of deeper personal relationships would stop as a result.

The last pictures
Two pictures of Father Anthony de Mello's last years spring up in the memory of those who came in contact with him. The first is that of a spiritual master, a rock of faith and a beacon of light for many. The second is that of a seeker for truth who, not satisfied with what he had experienced and built up, would relentlessly seek further.

Lonavla is linked in the consciousness of many to Father de Mello and to sadhana. It is from there that his name and fame had spread around the world. He travelled a lot in India, creating spiritual renewal in different communities of religious men and women. Travel took him to the South Asian countries, particularly to Japan, Malaysia and Singapore. He regularly visited America, where his 'satellite talks and retreats' had become quite popular. He was a master and guide to many who found his teachings to be a light and a solace, a newer and deeper vision of their Christian and religious life. He spoke and preached also to bishops, who highly esteemed and appreciated him.

But the Society of Jesus in India and elsewhere was also aware of his prophetic, sometimes critical attitude to what happens in the church. Some remarked sometimes jokingly about

ANTHONY DE MELLO

Rome taking him to task. But nobody sensed or raised doubts about his unconditional love and respect for the church, as a true Jesuit ought to be. For many individuals, he was a friend and master, generous not only in kind but sharing all that he possessed and, above all, generous in what people do not easily share: time. He spent almost every minute of it for others, as giving attention to others was his way of loving. One disciple joyfully remarks:

> Each time I was with Tony I was the only one who mattered to him. That was a great feeling. I could be just natural and free before him. I could speak with ease and share with him my most hidden thoughts. Nothing surprised him.
> (*We Heard the Bird Sing*, 2)

During the last years of his life, a rapid change came about in him. An intimate friend very closely watched this transformation. He quotes Tony: 'I feel as if I am forced to follow this new path from within, as if I am urged strongly to live only in the present.' (*We heard the Bird Sing*, 100). That feeling was the call to love in liberty and freedom unencumbered by the baggage of structures, rules and traditions. His former teaching on experience as more important than knowledge and on direct experience of God in prayer were now producing in him an urge for simplicity and freedom by continuously trying to find the essential, which is love, in all acts and relations. For example, to the friend who was not certain of this love and so asked him if there was place for emotional feelings, Tony replied:

> 'Yes, of course there is, my dear, otherwise life would be so dull. But there is no place for negative emotions – all that kind of suffering is really a waste of time and a waste of precious life. Negative emotions always come from our wrong perceptions and wrong ideas. But for positive emotions there is plenty of place: however, positive emotions that are aroused by present reality, not by past memories, because to return to the past is to return to what is dead.'
> (*We Heard the Bird Sing*, 104)

For Father de Mello, spirituality begins to appear where simplicity of life and nature become the natural way of life. In a letter of April 14, 1987, a few months before his death, he writes that:

> ... I am perfectly peaceful and content to be here in the cool of

the morning, gazing out of the window at the serenity of the scenery, the bright sunshine, the cool breeze, the young leaves sprouting in the trees and the clear blue sky. Everything is so soaked in peacefulness and life. That is the way our hearts should be as we go through life. I can sense that my heart is moving towards this, though there are so many mountain loads of rubbish and illusions to remove. I am happier than ever before in my life.'
(*We Heard the Bird Sing*, 113)

He always loved nature and its beauty, but now nature seemed to take a more direct place in his spiritual perception. One of his cherished spots for walks was Lonavla Lake. He would sit on the parapet of the bridge facing the sky beyond the lake and watch the sunset as though he was taking it in. On such an occasion he exhorts his companion:

'Do not verbalise the scene, Geeta,' a fiend of his recalls his words, 'just watch and let the colours come and go.' Or as another remembers: 'When I look at the horizon,' Tony said on a particular occasion, his eyes fixed on the distant scene, 'I think of creation. Time touches eternity. I wonder how many millions of sunsets this spot has witnessed.'
(*We Heard the Bird Sing*, 99)

This contemplation of the nature would take him to mystical heights:

I think of the life-force of countless people who have watched the sunsets before us, and of the millions who will do so after us. You and I are two insignificant yet infinitely precious particles in the heart of the universe that throbs with the heart of Christ. If people were to look at the infinity of space and allow their heart to be in tune with the universal soul, they would stop their savage hunt for power and wealth.
(*We Heard the Bird Sing*, 99)

Deep within him, he began to feel strongly what many of the Hindu and Buddhist masters felt in their lives as they neared to awakening: simplicity in renunciation. On 29 April 1987, a few weeks before he died, he answered to a letter requesting an appointment after his return from the USA: 'I don't know when or where we will meet; perhaps you will see me next, sitting under a bodhi tree naked and silent!' (*We Heard the Bird Sing*, 113). He was not merely 'cracking a joke' as, apparently, the thought of freedom and simplicity in life had taken him up.

In Tony's last letter of 1 June 1987, in the night he died, he writes the following: '... I find the whole of my interest is now focused on something else, on the 'world of the Spirit', and I see everything else as trifling and so irrelevant ... never before in my life have I felt so happy, so free ...' (*We Heard the Bird Sing*, 112-113).

The very Sadhana Institute he founded began to appear to him as a burden. He confides to one of his friends: 'I see the new sadhana building as my mausoleum. I know I will not live in it for long. I see it clearly. My life is coming to an end.' (*We Heard the Bird Sing*, 100). His friends attest to his desire to give up sadhana for the elite, that is, Jesuits and other religious men and women, and take it to the poor and simple of the world, in particular, to lay people in search of spiritual life and to the poor and uneducated of India and other countries. He wanted to bring them the message of liberation as many masters in Hinduism and Buddhism do, in simplicity, informally, in simple words and practices.

But was he feeling the premonitions of death? He was, on the whole, in good health, but certain signs of weakness were showing up in the form of difficulties with digestion, albino rash on the skin, an occasional irregularity in blood pressure. These illnesses sometimes worried him but he paid no great attention to them in his untiring activity. He writes on 14 April 1987, '... I am quite amazed that in spite of the work entailed in the renewal, I am not tired at all. I feel some kind of congestion in the chest. I wonder if that is what they call a chest cold. Anyway, except for that, I feel perfectly fit.' (*We Heard the Bird Sing*, 113)

But there was another experience he was feeling from time to time, an experience that surpassed the physical or psychic. The following is from a letter in early 1986:

... there are so many things I want to write about, but something has happened to me today and I just cannot write. Last night I had a horrible experience – one of the worst experiences of my life – and I could not sleep much. It would take too long to describe, but it was a kind of feeling of despair

and fright and a terrible loneliness ... as if nobody could reach me, no one could touch me, I was just abandoned by God and everyone. And I woke up with such a fright, sweating in spite of the intense cold, so I had to open the windows and walk up and down the room. If that despair had lasted longer I felt I would go mad. This morning I talked with someone about it. I feel it is some kind of spiritual experience ... The whole of today I have been feeling a kind of sadness and very tired and I was forcing myself to do the essential task that had to be done ... N.B. Please don't worry about my sadness – twice before I have had this kind of sadness ... and I have gradually grown out of it.
(*We Heard the Bird Sing*, 112)

Did such an experience bring on the massive and fatal heart attack on the night of 1 June 1987, at the Jesuit community in Fordham College? He had spent the previous week hard at work on the manuscript of his book *The Prayer of the Frog* in two volumes. He completed it and sent to the press. Before boarding the plane to New York, he spent the last day in India at his sister's house in Bandra, Mumbai. At the end of the meal, he remarked that he could not move his hands. After a rest, he was driven to the airport. Arriving in New York, he was met by his brother Bill who was there on business. He brought him to the Jesuit community and spent the evening with him. When he left him, Tony spent a few moments in the lounge with his Jesuit friends and retired to bed. He was found dead on the floor the next morning. Was that a death in sequel to intense activity and fatigue with premonitions of an imminent infarct? Or was it a mystical experience provoked by a call to love that his heart could not support?

His body was flown back to Mumbai and laid to rest at St Peter's Church in Bandra, the same church where he was baptised and ordained priest. On his tomb are engraved the words of Julian of Norwich, in which he saw the embodiment of the essence of his message:
All shall be well
And all shall be well
And all manner of thing shall be well

The tomb, unfortunately, is not visible today. The parish authorities have, for reasons unknown to me, covered the place with thick carpets and installed there, curiously at the very entrance of the church, the Blessed Sacrament exposed. Is this perhaps a way to stop devotions to Father de Mello because of the Roman *Notification*?

CHAPTER TWO

Spiritual teachings of Father Anthony de Mello

In his lifetime, Father Anthony de Mello did not structure or systematise his teachings on spirituality. His interest lay only in the art of living spirituality, experimenting and sharing it with others in the hope of awakening in them a taste for it. The framework in which he developed his spiritual outlook was highly therapeutic, that is, he invariably sought to heal religious men and women from unhealthy and oppressive psychological problems caused in them by an ill-conceived spiritual and human outlook in life. Furthermore, it was an ever-growing spirituality, like fermenting wine that is not supposed to be contained in closed, airtight vessels. Such a growth was visible in him up to the very end of his life. He used to tell his listeners that if they followed what he said, they did so at their own risk because he could change his views without notice. And that was not a mere joke. His friends recall how he tried spiritual experiments first on himself before proposing them to others. When he was convinced of the value of a spiritual practice, he would speak about it to others with a contagious conviction and zeal.

In fact, much of what is known about Father de Mello's spirituality are only aspects of spirituality in growth, which came to an end rather abruptly. During his life, two growths were taking shape in him: emotional and spiritual. They did not always go hand in hand. In his youth, Tony was a man of religious and spiritual certitudes, convinced of the rigid traditional practices of the Goan Catholic Church. These were not only confirmed but also somehow upheld by the Spanish Jesuits in Mumbai and the Spanish mystical spirituality he learnt later. Then, about the time he became a Jesuit priest, there came in him an awakening to the spirit of freedom, taking the form of liberation from deep-rooted tension, anguish and guilt linked with an oppressive idea of God. What is known of him is mostly the radiation of this liberation in its unfinished forms.

Father Rossi Rego SJ, one of Father de Mello's close students, whom de Mello sometimes sent out to replace him for retreats, once remarked to me in a personal conversation that:

> The seeds of his later development were already present in his earliest writings. For example, the Annual Retreat he gave to the Canossian Sisters in 1971 (tape-recorded and transcribed by one of the sisters), a retreat full of traditional Ignatian spirituality and Christian piety, already contains his idea of liberty as spiritual fulfilment, which he developed only later on and preached with conviction. He seems to have experienced a form of enlightenment that later on completely changed his attitude towards the rigid spirituality that he had practised up to that point. However, his emotional growth was not in measure to live and preach what he felt as enlightenment. This point is where he begins to show an interest in psychology.

(Communication recorded on 2.8.2005)

From then on, de Mello frequented schools of modern psychology in the United States and began to apply psychology to spirituality. The *Spiritual Exercises* of St Ignatius of Loyola that he regularly gave and the spiritual guidance he offered was full of psychology. This interest in psychology would lead him to other religions and other spiritualities, too, resulting in what he called sadhana. This newer approach to spiritual life brought him into contact with numerous Jesuits and other religious men and women, a contact that he sought and in which he experimented on the newly discovered paths of spiritual life. His work with lay people was limited to his Western audience composed of free thinking Christians and non-Christians. In this interaction, his spirit seemed to grow to dimensions wider than those of his own Jesuit Order and that of the Catholic Church. He spoke then of a universal spirituality, a spirituality acceptable to all. He would remark that a good spirituality, if it is good, should be good for all. On this point a certain tension with the present-day church authorities was inevitable.

However, one notices an effort to structure the spiritual thought in his book, *Sadhana – A Way to God*, (1978) and later in a short article he wrote for the journal *Concilium* (1982: 'An

Eastern Christian Speaks of Prayer). But scarcely had these works appeared, than de Mello was not at ease with them, because his spiritual consciousness had already outgrown these written forms. He felt that spirituality could not be contained in a series of 'exercises'. Furthermore, written words were not the final expression for him. On the contrary, the power lay in the spoken word – the living word that creates life here and now. The only form of expression in which he found satisfaction was stories, parables and living metaphors that contained truth but which did not bind it to words, yielding a continuous growth of meaning.

Anthony de Mello's spirituality is, therefore, marked by different stages. At each stage he puts forth convincing arguments. However, it would be a mistake to fix him to just one of these stages. Let us take, for example, his idea of prayer. Initially, in his youth, prayer meant for him what the Catholic Church and the Jesuits of Mumbai taught as prayer: seeking union with God through mental and vocal prayers. He practised and preached it with great conviction. But, at a later stage, prayer meant for him the awareness with which one looks at reality outside oneself and inside oneself. Finally, in the last stage of his life, prayer was, for him, a life led in a spirit of liberty and happiness. The latter stages were not deviations from the earlier but a fuller and better understanding of prayer, the heart raising to higher mystical states – what his spiritual master, Ignatius of Loyola, taught as the crown of his *Spiritual Exercises*: Contemplation for obtaining love, namely, seeing God in all things and at all moments in daily life.

People who heard him and followed him often had difficulty passing from one stage to another. Some of them came to him to learn prayer but were somewhat dismayed to see that he served instead, awareness. 'Where is prayer in all this?' they would ask. However, a later stage did not mean a negation of the previous. Father de Mello respected people at their own spiritual level. He would sometimes say that when he gave a conference, he gave, in fact, a hundred conferences because each of the hundred persons who listened to him had a confirmation of their own spiritual stage of life. He seemed to be at home with people of all stages of spiritual progress. He never imposed a form but always showed the way to go ahead and deepen the experience. He never belittled the simple spirituality of simple people. Simple vocal prayer, litanies and recitation of the rosary, for example, always remained dear to him, just as the mystical heights gained through awareness.

However, today, almost twenty years after his death, there are sufficient documents and testimonies of people to gain insight into his spiritual teachings which permit us to draw an outline of his spirituality. Two approaches, among others, are possible. One can trace the growth of his spirituality through a chronological study of his writings. Another way is through a study of his stories and the spiritual themes underlying them. I have not gone into a chronological dating and study of his writings. This work, to my knowledge, remains to be done. Neither have I done the thematic study of his stories and parables. The outline I draw here is a synthesis, in the first place, of what I learned from Tony through my contacts with him, what I heard and lived with him. Secondly, I have read his writings over and over again and meditated with and upon them. An outline of this spirituality became clear to me through the experience I gained in sadhanas which I conduct regularly since the death of Father de Mello, for people of different walks of life in Switzerland, France, Belgium, Germany and sometimes in Canada. My academic profession – the study of religions – has further permitted me to compare Father de Mello's teachings with those of the great religions of the world and glean therein a certain structure underlying the spiritual experience.

An outline of Father de Mello's spirituality
I am fully aware of the risks involved in undertaking a summary of Father de Mello's spirituality. For, although the 'Rolling Stone' has now come to a standstill, de Mello's teachings continue to roll on in the hearts and minds of his students and his readers, in different ways and manners that cannot be easily put down on paper. The following summary is simply my personal view. It has proved its worth for several people. It might help to get a coherent idea of de Mello's teachings. Needless to say, I am open to all criticism and suggestions in order to improve upon this outline.

SPIRITUAL TEACHINGS

Father de Mello's spirituality is a process of awakening to happiness and ultimately to freedom. It can be outlined in four steps:
1. Happiness is the goal in life. But, instead, many experience only suffering.
2. The cause of suffering is attachment; that is, happiness sought through conditions.
3. There is a way out: detachment through discernment.
4. Happiness is freedom.

1. HAPPINESS IS THE GOAL IN LIFE. BUT, INSTEAD, MANY EXPERIENCE ONLY SUFFERING.

All human beings have happiness as their ultimate goal in life. Even though this idea is often developed only by philosophers and saints, the experience of it belongs to one and all. Behind all human strivings – great and small, individual and social – happiness is sought as the end. As such, it is the motivating force of all human deeds. Happiness is often conceived as the fulfilment of one's aims and expectations, that is, what an individual sets for his life, what he expects from others and what others expect from him. Success in happiness is declared to be the crown of life. Individuals and society are evaluated by the level of success they achieve. That is also the ideal model set by our educational systems and societies. That type of success in life is the acquired happiness.

But there is another happiness that is not acquired. It happens. It is the true happiness. It is not what one can buy with success in wealth and power. So, luckily, it is not confined only to the rich and successful. In fact, happiness is not the characteristic mark of the rich and the so-called developed and powerful nations of the world. The latter are in fact in need of happiness as much as others, if not more. Simple joy in life, a welcoming heart and contentment seem to disappear where material wealth accumulates. Frustration, depression and suicides are frequent where people seemingly have everything in abundance.

Acquired happiness
The acquired happiness is that which is obtained through efforts and possessions, through pleasures of body and mind (food,

pleasures and sex), through recognition and renown. But it is our common experience that this type of happiness is transitory and fleeting – it quickly passes away, creating a renewed void and thirst for more. And when this thirst is not satisfied, frustration and inner gnawing sets in, making life less interesting. *Amour est comme une cigarette* ('Love is like a cigarette'), sang a French singer. When one cigarette is smoked, the hand goes in for another until smoking itself becomes unbearable torture. But not for long. It starts again.

Father de Mello's concept of suffering takes into account the distinction made in Eastern religions between suffering and pain. Pain is different from suffering. Pain is inevitable in life; it is necessary for life and its growth; it is part of life's process and adventure. It is only through painful movements that a child learns to walk. It is through the pains of hunger that the body is built up. Adults know the value of pain while trying to jog and while doing different physical exercises which build the body and bring it into a state of well being. In modern cities, while walking on the pavements, one's attention can often be drawn to certain lighted basements where huge 'instruments of torture' are installed and to which people young and old, men and women, betake themselves with joy, paying a rather high fee for the painful activity which is called 'bodybuilding'.

Suffering, on the other hand, is something that is incompatible with life. It is the inner gnawing of the spirit that steadily tortures and diminishes life and kills it little by little. It is extremely negative and destructive. It has to be avoided, uprooted and eliminated. People often mistake one for the other, pain for suffering. Many experiences in life, which are solely of a painful nature, are interpreted as suffering. One can learn to go through pain joyfully, but not through suffering, which is incompatible with joy.

Some of Tony's friends testify to what they often heard from him:
> 'Pain is neither positive nor negative: pain is of life. And life is growth and any growth has pain as one of its essential ingredients.'
> 'If I immunise myself by all means against pain, then I will be shutting myself from intimacy and growth, from life itself.'

'It's painful and I can take it, is a life-giving attitude.'
'You can comply and have no pain, and be dead: You can be free and spontaneous and have pain and be alive.'
Once I realised that I need not avoid pain at all costs, I began to breathe more freely. I felt at ease to explore the pains of my life, like the separation of my parents. I recognised the energy being released if only I learn to accept the inevitable and the factors over which I have no control. With Tony pointing out this truth at crucial and vulnerable moments and later becoming aware of it by myself, I was led to explore and 'thaw out' the 'frozen areas' of my life. They began to have life and movement again.
(*We Heard the Bird Sing*, 11)

Furthermore, pain in all its forms, physical as well as psychological (the loss of a beloved for example) come to us from outside; it is not of our making. On the contrary, suffering is what arises from within. It is shocking to discover that way that I am the sole cause of my suffering because it is I who give vent to it. I am the sole person who battles against something undesired. I am frustrated at not succeeding to possess that which I desire and that which I consider to be the object of my striving, or that which I try to shun or keep away from me. There is no such thing as suffering outside; no suffering anywhere except in my individual spirit in turmoil. Naturally, such a suffering spirit provokes suffering in others. Hate, vengeance and wars, destruction and killings are the expressions of spirits in suffering. These actions in themselves are not evil but the spirit that provokes it is. Here lies a subtle but none the less important distinction that has to be made between pain and suffering.

Hunger, famine and death are all in fact pains, but expressions of life and its process. It all depends how one looks at them. The master and the disciple, so goes one of de Mello's stories, began to fast together because the country was under duress. After forty days, the master became enlightened. The neighbour, however, was dead! There's also another story about the young man who fell down with a thud in the garden from the window that he was painting. A woman came running to help and exclaimed, 'Boy, the fall was painful, wasn't it?' To which he replied, 'No, Madam, not the fall but the impact!'

Many people experience pains in life as a chain of suffering because they do not know the art of accepting them as just that; they revolt against them. There are others who create and propagate sufferings, getting out of them secret pleasures, a certain satisfaction in the sufferings of others. But the form of suffering that is common is in those who settle down to a life of small joys and satisfactions, contenting themselves with their little possessions, taking them to be the ultimate happiness that one can hope for in life. They are those who were born in a prison cell, grew up in it and die in it. They never experience the true happiness which is their birthright. They have absolutely no inkling of it. They don't even know that they suffer. Father de Mello has a beautiful story to depict such a suffering:

A man found an eagle's egg and put it in the nest of a backyard hen. The eagle hatched with the brood of chicks and grew up with them.

All his life the eagle did what the backyard chickens did, thinking he was a backyard chicken. He scratched the earth for worms and insects. He clucked and cackled. And he would thrash his wings and fly a few feet into the air like the chickens. After all, that is how a chicken is supposed to fly, isn't it?

Years passed and the eagle grew very old. One day he saw a magnificent bird far above him in the cloudless sky. It floated in graceful majesty among the powerful wind currents, with scarcely a beat of its strong golden wings.

The eagle looked up in awe. 'Who's that?' he said to his neighbour.

'That's the eagle, the king of the birds,' said his neighbour. 'But don't give it another thought. You and I are different from him.'

So the eagle never gave it another thought. He died thinking he was a backyard chicken.
(*The Song of the Bird*, 120-121)

Happiness for the eagle is not the drab, though carefree life of the backyard, but flying in the boundless blue skies.

The worst suffering is not to know and not to experience what true happiness is:

Most people, even though they don't know it, are asleep. They're born asleep, they live asleep, they marry in their sleep, they breed children in their sleep, they die in their sleep without ever waking up. They never understand the loveliness and the beauty of this thing that we call human existence.
(*Awareness*, 5)

Real happiness
The goal of life is happiness. So, too, is the goal of spirituality. Happiness not just after death in what is believed to be eternity, but here and now in the present. A spirituality that does not lead to joy, peace, contentment, compassion and thanksgiving is not a true spirituality. But what is this happiness? A utopian concept? Many would wonder if such a state exists at all. Evidently, this happiness is not the one that is acquired through one's efforts. It is a gift that is given at all times and in all places, but not accepted by all. For it requires opening one's eyes and seeing it. It is like the sun shining, but those who sleep or close their eyes cannot see it. Happiness is not what one can buy with money or power. It is a state of mind and body in which one experiences peace, joy, contentment, love, compassion and thanksgiving – all in one. It is what Jesus says: 'Peace is what I leave with you; it is my own peace that I give you; I do not give it as the world does. Do not be worried and upset; do not be afraid.' (John 16:27). Only when one experiences this gift does one realise that it comes as a pure grace, a pure gift.

In his *Spiritual Exercises*, Ignatius of Loyola spoke of the greater glory of God as the goal of spiritual life. The Eastern religions have developed concepts of the liberated state (*moksha* or *nirvana*) which, in their content, are akin to what Jesus speaks of as 'the kingdom of God' or the 'reign of God'. It is that which St Augustine alludes to when he says: 'Our hearts are made for thee, O Lord, and they are restless until they rest contented in thee.' Like the kingdom of God, happiness is here and now, but grows to its plenitude in fullness of time.

2. The cause of suffering is attachment; that is, happiness sought through conditions.

Suffering, that ungodly gnawing state of mind which destroys our body and spirit, a state that squanders the gift of God that is life, has a cause, the only cause that is wholly and solely responsible for it: attachment.

Attachment does not mean the joy of life in enjoying good food and drinks, the pleasure of work and hobby, the company of one's family, the joy of being husband and wife, the pleasures experienced with children, friends or lover. Attachment is not the joy that one experiences in relationships or in friendships. Attachment is not the pleasure experienced in sexual life. Attachment is also not the comforts of life that one might have the chance to experience.

Attachment is, in the first place, the craving for possessing or also the craving for shunning something or somebody; and to make of this craved reality the condition for one's happiness. Thus, for example, people seek to be happy by possessing wealth ... or such and such a person ... or such and such a state of life. They set those realities as condition for their happiness. People, in fact, do not want to be just happy; they want to be happy only according to their models of happiness and according to their expectations; their desires formed by themselves or by others through appropriation of wealth, fame, power and so forth.

Possession or appropriation is the common form of attachment. But there is another more subtle form of possession or appropriation: rejection. Our attachment then is to that state of life where the undesired object is seen to be eliminated. The shunning of it becomes a condition for happiness: 'I cannot be happy so long as my mother is bedridden,' 'I cannot be happy as long as my wife does not live up to my social status ...' or 'I can be happy only when I get rid of a particular duty' and so forth.

Such attachments, or conditions put for happiness, are the real root causes of all suffering. Happiness sought in this manner is impermanent and fleeting. It asks for more. And there being naturally limits put by nature or by others to this frantic craving, suffering begins to rise in the consciousness. It gnaws and eats up from within. One of Father de Mello's stories, one among many others, illustrates this point very well. It is like the little fish that frantically looks for the 'ocean' in the midst of the water; when another fish tells it that it swims right in the ocean, the little fish is dismayed: 'What! That is the ocean? No, it's just water' and swims elsewhere to seek the ocean (*The Song of the Bird*, 14-15). We are in fact surrounded by happiness; we swim in it. But it does not correspond to our expectations and so the craving is directed elsewhere. The fish appears again, now in human form; it seeks not Ocean but God. He does not find him in nature nor among living beings. So, frustrated, goes elsewhere to seek him. The seeking becomes more important for him than finding – like a religious who adores more his rules than the One to whom the rules should lead.

The base on which our society and educational systems are constructed is precisely this craving. From it arises a network of attachments. Life is programmed through such attachments in the form of expectations: expectations towards oneself and towards others, and expectations of others towards oneself and towards one's life. Such a network of attachments, the conditioning and the programming in which we try to find meaning for our life and its fulfilment, render happiness impossible. The programming and conditionings clash with one another in our inter-personal societal relationships. From suffering within, they also provoke suffering without. Wars are born this way in the hearts of people. Let's read de Mello:

> Do you see now how you are in a prison created by the beliefs and traditions of your society and culture and by the ideas, prejudices, attachments and fears of your past experiences?
>
> Wall upon wall surrounds your prison cell so that it seems almost impossible that you will ever break out and make contact with the richness of life and love and freedom that lies beyond your prison fortress. And yet the task, far from being impossible, is actually easy and delightful.
> (*Call to Love*, 32-33)

True happiness is not what one enjoys when one's expectations are fulfilled. Happiness is not linked to achievements. Happiness is a state of being, a deep feeling of peace, joy, love, contentment and compassion that invades us for no reason at all. It is like light that enters the room when the shutters are opened. Happiness is not achieved but something to which one is awakened.

In fact, it is a state that is present at all times and in all places, but most of the people are unable to experience it because they do not see it. They look elsewhere. What they try to see is not happiness but the *idea* of happiness which they crave for. They do not recognise it because it does not resemble that which they are seeking. This inability to see and enjoy happiness where life takes place, makes the human person restless. All ideas and expectations of happiness do bring a dose of thrill, which quickly vanishes, leaving the person to seek more and more.

3. THERE IS A WAY OUT: DETACHMENT THROUGH DISCERNMENT

How to get out of this prison and how to go to the root cause of suffering? No remedy to alleviate suffering and no soothing techniques of prayer and ritual can be of real help. Often, the spiritual counsels given in Christianity or in other religions to suffering persons are pain-killers and analgesics. They do not help to root out the cause of suffering. Pious counsels like 'Offer it all to God through communion with the sufferings of the Crucified Lord' might bring some momentary consolation to the suffering soul. But unless the root cause is weeded out, no lasting relief can be had. The true and only help that one can offer to a suffering person is to make him or her see that which really provokes suffering: the attachment. As Father de Mello says:

> The only way someone can be of help to you is in challenging your ideas. If you're ready to listen and if you're ready to be challenged, there's one thing that you can do, but no one can help you. What is this most important thing of all? It's called self-observation.
> (*Awareness*, 35-36)

That is the first step towards the discernment: the root cause of suffering lies in the person that suffers and not outside him or her: attachment or craving to possess or shun. The fall of attachment is the state of detachment.

What is detachment?

Detachment does not mean apathy or indifference. A detached person, as he or she is often described in spiritual texts, is not someone become indifferent to pleasures or pains, someone who shows distaste for life and its pleasures. A detached person is a free person. He or she enjoys everything and every moment in life. However, his joy and happiness are no longer determined by the object of desires. There is joy in possessing them, but there is also joy when he does not possess them. If success brings pleasure, failure will not be a lesser occasion for happiness. The detached person is happy with things and persons which people call beautiful; but his joy is no less in things and in people whom society as a whole judges ugly and repugnant. The detached person feels intensely the pain of injustice meted out in life: hunger and thirst of the poor, violence and wars shake him up and produce intense pain in him. But he or she does not suffer, that is, he or she is not in despair or hope-less about this. In the attitude and judgement of this person there is no hate, revenge or frustration. The peace and happiness of detachment is, in fact, detached from the object in question. The inner consolation in joy or in pain rises from some other source.

Like attachment, the term 'detachment' also evokes images of passivity, disinterest or indifference. However, detachment is just the contrary. Only the detached person, in fact, is capable of true dynamic action of the fullest choice. Religious traditions have often mistakenly projected the image of a detached saint as someone cut out from life's force and interest; a person to be kept high up on the altar, unsullied from involvement in life. Father de Mello loved to quote a verse from the *Bhagavad Gita* (I, 21), in which the warrior, Arjuna, bids his charioteer to drive his chariot right into the din of the battle. That is the image of a detached person; a person who is capable of relating himself fully to life's forces, because he is free from all attachments. He poses no conditions for happiness. The detached person does not *seek* happiness; he *experiences* happiness in all situations of life. He is totally free to delve deeply into life which is, for him, a continuous grace and gift from God.

Detachment, therefore, means the inner capacity to experience happiness (we might call it here God) in everything.

Opening one's heart and soul to happiness with whatever life's situation or reality one comes into contact. Detachment means the capacity to experience happiness in all conditions:
> Traveller: 'What kind of weather are we going to have today?'
> Shepherd: 'The kind of weather I like.'
> 'How do you know it will be the kind of weather you like?'
> 'Having found out, sir, that I cannot always get what I like, I have learnt always to like what I get. So I am quite sure we will have the kind of weather I like.'

And Tony comments:
> Happiness and unhappiness are in the way we meet events, not in the nature of those events themselves.
> (*The Prayer of the Frog II*, 235)

It is certainly a joy to possess a fine, beautiful car; but can the loss of it by stealth or accident also be a moment of joy? That will be the test of detachment. It is perfectly okay to expect, on a given occasion, a good dinner; but will happiness disappear if one were served only a scrambled egg or a plate of lentils or even made to depart with a hungry stomach? In the state of detachment, one discovers that happiness is present at all moments and in all times and that only one's attachments hide it from one's eyes.

Discernment

Seeing one's attachments is the fundamental act of discernment. Anthony de Mello gave the highest priority in his spiritual teachings to the art of discernment. In other words, he was interpreting the 'Principle and Foundation' and the 'Discernment of the spirits' of the *Spiritual Exercises* of Ignatius of Loyola. For Ignatius, a man of discernment was a free man to whom one could entrust any job, regardless of the level of responsibility, without hesitation. Nothing was to be dangerous to a man of discernment. Ignatius' concept of detachment or 'indifference,' as he calls it, takes on a deeper meaning when seen in the light of the Buddhist and Hindu concepts of discernment (*viveka*), where indifference does not mean apathy towards things and beings. It is becoming aware of one's attachments and how they influence one's thinking and actions creating a programmation and conditioning with which one seeks the meaning of one's life and fulfilment.

According to the Eastern religions, discernment is not just a mental, rational activity, that is, analysis, comparison and evaluation leading to decisions. These religions consider one's mental faculty so tarnished by attachments and subdued to work within programmations, that it is practically incapable of making selfless judgements or choices. Discernment, therefore, is the awakening of the heart. It is the act of seeing, understanding and experiencing.

Evidently, the heart does not awaken through mental activity but through the calming of the whole human person. 'The Chinese sage, Lao-tse, says, "Muddy water, let stand, becomes clear".' (*Wellsprings*, 273) In other words, where self-observation or awareness is practised, spirituality is not experienced as achievement but as a discovery: discovering the reality that comes into being and that unfolds like a flower blossoming and giving off its fragrance. Sanctity is not the result of hard mental effort or determination of willpower. Sainthood is witnessing the marvels of God, the wonders that God has done. It is the thanksgiving that sprouts in the heart after the example of Mary: 'My heart praises the Lord; my soul is glad because of God my Saviour, for he has remembered me, his lowly servant! From now on all people will call me happy, because of the great things the Mighty God has done for me. His name is holy.' (Lk 1:46-49)

In all his sadhanas, Anthony de Mello was teaching his audience the art of discerning the play of human mind and spirit, the perception of the subtle games of attachment that the conscience plays and the power of the detached, free state. Becoming aware of attachments is already the threshold of detachment and of happiness. His two books, *Awareness* and *Call to Love*, are splendid teachings of this aspect of spiritual life. He was perfectly aware of the necessity of giving clear guidelines in this matter of discernment, failing which the spiritual edifice would necessarily come down, built as it is on sand. The free man and the state of liberty, which were to be the end result of spirituality, were possible only when the person was capable of clear discernment.

One sees today in this contemporary world how the different

new religious movements and groups often come to a sad downfall precisely because they have no clear teaching on discernment. And this downfall is coming at a peculiar time when people have to live their spiritual freedom on their own, unable to find experienced masters.

Concretely, what is a detached state of mind? Father de Mello explains this beautifully in the first meditation in *Call to Love*:

> Recall the kind of feeling you have when someone praises you, when you are approved, accepted, applauded. And contrast that with the kind of feeling that arises within you when you look at the sunset or the sunrise, or nature in general or when you read a book or watch a movie that you thoroughly enjoy. Get the taste of this feeling.
>
> And contrast it with the first, namely, the one that was generated within you when you were praised. Understand that the first type of feeling comes from self-glorification, self-promotion. It is a worldly feeling. The second comes from self-fulfilment, a soul-feeling.
>
> (*Call to Love*, 1)

Approval, acceptance, applause, the feeling of success, getting to the top, the feeling of power are all situations of attachment, that is, conditions through which one seeks happiness and has the feeling of acquiring it. On the other hand, the enjoyment of a sunset or sunrise, the enjoyment of a wonderful symphony, the joy in absorbing oneself in a hobby, the joy of friendship, intimacy and companionship are examples of detachment because there are no conditions put there for happiness. One does not determine how happiness should be or should take place; the person is just engrossed in happiness in these situations. Spirituality is the experiencing of this joy of life: awakening to life with a continual act of thanksgiving rising from the heart.

Jesuits and other religious persons who came to Father de Mello were often suffering from an ill-conceived concept of sanctity which brought upon them, on their body, stifling tensions, and feelings of guilt in their mind. Father de Mello compared their state of life to a desert where everything was dry because the source of life, water, was not available. The first thing to revive such persons was to awaken in them a taste of life through the awakening of their senses. I remember how Tony once gave advice to a young Jesuit tortured by fear and guilt in his spiritual life: 'You should start by pampering your senses, like a mother pampers a baby. Seek and give pleasure to your senses.' When the young man complained that, in the Jesuit house (De Nobili College), there were not many things to pamper the senses, Tony suggested that he go to Bombay regularly on the weekends and enjoy nice food in restaurants, films in cinema houses and so enjoy a fine time. However shocking such spiritual advice might appear, it was Tony's opinion that a good spirituality could not be built up in a body whose senses were dried and atrophied. Of course, pampering the senses cannot be a permanent rule or the end of spirituality, but it is a first step. Only in a healthy body and mind can true detachment take place.

Father de Mello's sadhana is precisely this experimentation in detachment. Spirituality meant growing in the joy of life unhindered by preconceived ideas of how happiness should be or should take place. For the detached person, nature is a joy, and so are all the activities of human beings and all creatures that live on this world. The pleasure of life and also the hardships of life – pain (but not suffering) and human relationships, including sexual ones – can be moments of deep detachment.

However, spiritual life in reality is not as simple as it might appear. The attachments cling to the innermost core of the being, and detachment from them can be a long process. Discernment is not an easy task. It takes place often only after several downfalls and moments of suffering. What is the remedy suggested here to come to the realisation of such a discernment? What is the method of Father de Mello?

Discernment through awareness
Father de Mello brings into his spiritual practice an element to which the old religions have accorded great importance, and to which also certain schools of modern psychology pay attention: awareness. The occidental Christian spiritualities do not seem to develop it in their practices. We have noted above the saying of Lao-tse: 'Muddy water, let stand, becomes clear.' Awareness is

comparable to the rays of the sun, which purify waters flowing on the earth, or burn out impurities, even produce fire when these rays converge under a magnifying glass. The yoga-master, Patanjali, defined yoga as the calming of all activities of mind (*citta-v.rtti-nirodha*) through awareness (*ekaagrataa*, literally 'one-pointedness'). The Buddhists have developed several methods of meditation based on the act of awareness (*vipassanaa, satipa.t.thana, zazen* etc.). In Christianity too one can notice the importance given to it by Jesus who concludes his teaching on the parable of Ten Girls: 'Be on your guard, then, because you do not know the day or the hour' (Mt 25:13). Or his earnest request to his disciples in moments of agony: 'Keep watch and pray that you will not fall into temptation. The spirit is willing, but the flesh is weak.' (Mt 26:41)

Awareness is the activity of focusing all attention of mind and body on one object. This object can be a concrete thing or a person. In addition, it can be an idea or an imaginary figure or symbol or a word repeated attentively. In short, it is any activity done with full attention. It is not so much the objects or their innate qualities that count but the power of the awareness brought on the spot. The results can be astonishing. This psychosomatic act can touch the spirit, awaken different states of consciousness and provoke deep sentiments. The idea behind awareness is that, when the whole conscious attention is focused on an object for a certain length of time, the state of consciousness changes and is gradually awakened to mystical states. Through awareness, the 'heart' opens; the curtains of illusions that bar our vision are torn down. The conscious state, thus awakened, would bring forth an experience of peace, joy, contentment, compassion, love and happiness. The human states of consciousness meet the divine. The direct contemplation of the Divine sets in.

It is understandable that the Christian conscience, particularly in the Latin Church and in Protestantism, can be somewhat uneasy at this practice and its use in Christian spirituality. Awareness might appear as an attempt to move the divine with human effort. Certainly there is human effort there. But that is only an effort to be awake, to be conscious of God's action. Without such a readiness ('Watch, therefore, for you do not know on what day your Lord is coming' Mt 24:42) even God's grace is hapless. One has got to be awake to enable God to act. Elsewhere, Father de Mello explains it humorously through a story:

'Is there anything I can do to make myself Enlightened?'
'As little as you can do to make the sun rise in the morning.'
'Then of what use are the spiritual exercises you prescribe?'
'To make sure you are not asleep when the sun begins to rise.'
(*One Minute Wisdom*, 10)

I think on this point of awareness lies the whole force and efficacy of Father de Mello's sadhana. This is how, through the act of awareness, spiritual pursuits can become enjoyable and easy, the spiritual journey adventurous and exciting.

Awareness itself is only a means, a technique that leads to something that is important and essential: the mystical experience. This experience is brought about not through the force of the technique but through the opening of the heart. One cannot stop short at the technique but at what results. Father de Mello explains further in his book, *Sadhana – A Way to God*:

A Jesuit friend who loves to dabble in such things (and, I suspect, test all religious theories with a healthy measure of scepticism) assures me that, through constantly saying to himself 'one-two-three-four' rhythmically, he achieves the same mystical results that his more religious confrères claim to achieve through the devout and rhythmical recitation of some ejaculation!' (29)

The awareness that the person exercises through meditations (Father de Mello suggests a number of such meditations in his books, *Sadhana – A Way to God* and *Wellsprings*) gives rise to a process, a sort of journeying from the external to the interior world. Concretely, awareness means to observe, to be aware of all details and aware of the object one contemplates. It means to observe an object with attention, without bringing in one's own personal judgement over it, or one's desire to change it, measure its worth or use to one's self. It is the pure act of seeing things as they are. This conscious state is not static. Awareness leads to the inner discovery that all things are in the process of becoming and that everything has a beginning, a moment of becoming, and an end; the whole world is transitory and flows like a river. There arises in this awareness a moment of void where the object disappears. When the meditating subject comes back to his normal consciousness, there is often a rush of joy and astonishment; a moment of happiness or, better, awareness of happiness. That is where the 'heart', that is the inner faculty in the human person, opens to experience God directly, unlike our other faculties that perceive him only through screens and shadows (cf *Sadhana – A Way to God*, 25-26).

In Father de Mello's meditations and teachings, awareness is practised in different stages with corresponding experiences of spiritual consolation. During the first stage, awareness of all the senses is focused on the object contemplated, thereby resulting in body and in mind in a certain calmness leading to a silence from within. The observation is intensified in the second stage. During it, one tries not to judge the object contemplated, that's to say, not to reject it or be attached to it depending on one's likes or dislikes, but contemplating it as it is. From such awareness results a deeper equanimity and a certain joy from within. During the third stage, the awareness listens to the object, dialogues with it in silence; evocations may rise within one's own depths of being. The ensuing sentiments are often feelings of union with the object and a sentiment of love. During the fourth stage, awareness brings silence, that is, the object contemplated disappears and the whole mind remains objectless, a state of consciousness often observed only after the end of the meditation and particularly through the depth of consolation, that is, experience through intense peace, joy and love.

Father de Mello, as we have noted before, rarely binds himself to formal methods or structures in his teachings or in his meditations. However, he seems to make an effort to be precise and methodical in his meditations in *Call to Love* where the steps noted above are perceivable in different meditations leading to a profound discernment.

4. Happiness is Freedom

Later in his life, Father de Mello preferred to call the spiritual goal as 'liberty' rather than 'happiness'. He realised that the word 'happiness' was somewhat distasteful to the modern man to whom it appears as utopia, a reality inaccessible in life. Or some people misunderstand it, as it is often the case in life that people take it to mean what we termed earlier *acquired pleasures*. He preferred to call this highest spiritual state 'liberty': 'Think of happiness as a state of inner liberty. Forget the word happiness altogether. Substitute it with 'inner liberty'. Inner liberty is true happiness.' (*We Heard the Bird Sing*, 72) He further develops this concept in his book *Call to Love*, where the theme of kingdom is repeatedly brought in line with the liberty to which the human being is called. Liberty is the crowning point of spiritual life. That is the inner liberty which enables a person to marvel at creation, wonder at beings and be ever thankful to God for his continuous grace that he showers on his creatures in the reality which is the present, here and now. That is salvation and liberation; not just what one achieves after life but what one begins in the here and now, when one sees life as a wellspring of joy and love. It is the sense of marvel; marvelling like a child:

> 'This is the prerogative of the child. He is so often in a state of wonder. So he is naturally at home in the kingdom of heaven.' (*The Song of the Bird*, 19)

The predominant sentiment of the person who comes into this state of consciousness is of thanksgiving. He or she feels that everything in life has been a grace and a gift, and that he has absolutely done nothing to deserve this gift. Everything in life appears to be important, great, wonderful, but nothing seems to be indispensable in comparison to the gift received; nothing is binding, nothing is important: *Solo Dios, basta* (Only God, that is enough) as Teresa of Avila would exclaim.

Father de Mello finds no words to describe this state of freedom. He speaks of it rather in stories and parables:

Uwais, the Sufi, was once asked:
'What did Grace bring you?'
He replied:
'When I wake in the morning I feel like a man who is not sure

he will live till evening.'
Said the questioner:
'But don't all men know this?'
Said Uwais:
'They certainly do. But not all of them feel it.'

And Father de Mello comments:
No one ever became drunk on an intellectual understanding of the word *wine*.
(*The Song of the Bird*, 3)

Tasting this great gift of freedom, one is no longer attached to things in life: 'If you knew the gift of God' (John 4:10). This experience of happiness as freedom creates a taste for renunciation, repentance, poverty and love:

The sannyasi [a Hindu renunciate] had reached the outskirts of the village and settled down under a tree for the night when a villager came running up to him and said, 'The stone! The stone! Give me the precious stone!'

'What stone?' asked the sannyasi.

'Last night the Lord Shiva appeared to me in a dream,' said the villager, 'and told me that if I went to the outskirts of the village at dusk I should find a sannyasi who would give me a precious stone that would make me rich forever.'

The sannyasi rummaged in his bag and pulled out a stone. 'He probably meant this one,' he said, as he handed the stone over to the villager. 'I found it on a forest path some days ago. You can certainly have it.'

The man looked at the stone in wonder. It was a diamond. Probably the largest diamond in the whole world for it was as large as a man's head.

He took the diamond and walked away. All night he tossed about in bed, unable to sleep. Next day at the crack of dawn he woke the sannyasi and said, 'Give me the wealth that makes it possible for you to give this diamond away so easily.'
(*The Song of the Bird*, 182-183)

Father de Mello's meditations, *Wellsprings*, are all marvellous examples of the person who has reached this state of liberty and

SPIRITUAL TEACHINGS

who looks at life and lives it in detachment, and so in freedom. People whose attachments are fallen begin to see life through the eyes of peace, joy, compassion, love and even happiness. However, Father de Mello wisely cautions:

> After enlightenment nothing really changes. Everything remains the same. Only now your heart is full of wonder. The tree is still a tree; and people are just what they were before; and so are you; and life goes on no differently. You may be as moody or even-tempered, just as wise or foolish as before. There's one major difference: now you see all these things with a different eye. You are more detached from it all. And your heart is full of wonder.
> (*The Song of the Bird*, 18-19)

The great change that can come over a spiritual person is not that he feels he begins to change the world, but that he begins to see the world through new eyes.

CONCLUDING REMARKS: SPIRITUALITY WITHOUT JESUS CHRIST?

This brief outline probably raises more questions than answers. The major difficulty at this point is to express in words what is felt deeply from within. It is a spiritual experience, comparable to the experience of love, which can be lived and experienced but which cannot be adequately put forth in written words.

What strikes me in the first place is the similarity between this resumé of Father de Mello's spirituality and the Four Noble Truths, the summary of Buddha's teachings. I do not think that Father de Mello, in spite of the fact that he was deeply influenced by the Buddhist approach, intended to copy this great Indian master. The similarity is inevitable, because almost all the great spiritualities have this fundamental scheme of transiting from impurity to purity, from prison to freedom, from sin to salvation. The four-fold path of the Yogasuutra of Patanjali, whose spiritual genius is discovered today more and more in the schools of yoga and sometimes in psychology, is again structured on the same model. Jesus' teachings on the kingdom are not exceptions: the need of repentance, that is recognition and admission that we are in sin, the growth in the kingdom and its final fulfilment. What Christian mysticism has, summarised in *via purgativa, via illumnativa* and *via unitiva,* implies the same vision of life: marching from the world of suffering through discernment and purification to the world where suffering has no place because everything is filled by the abundance of God.

We will have opportunities to review this summary and bring to it more elements against the background of the critique made by the Roman *Notification* which will be our subject in the following chapter.

A Christian is certainly perplexed at the idea to see that, in the four summarised points, Father de Mello's spirituality has apparently no place for Jesus Christ. One might ask if this then is a Christian spirituality. Well, the absence of Jesus Christ, as we shall remark in the following pages, is only apparent. In fact, Jesus Christ occupies the central place in his thought. Father de Mello was preaching to his Jesuit brethren and to other religious men and women whose spirituality was already steeped in christology. What they needed was not so much a discourse about Jesus Christ but a spiritual outlook in life that was certainly Christ-centred but not explicitly and verbally bringing in christological terms. The religious needed more an awakening in their human life.

On one occasion, after a sadhana I conducted in Paris, I had the very joyful experience of listening to a testimony of the discovery of the Christ-centredness of sadhana. It was a weekend organised for yoga teachers in France. None of them were church-goers or had clear ideas about their Christianity. However, they were all taken up by the spirituality of Father de Mello and the practice of the sadhana. During the whole weekend I did not mention a word about Jesus Christ. But, at the end of the sadhana, as we were taking our farewells, a woman came to me to thank me for the sadhana I gave. She said that she was not a Christian but she felt the strong presence of Jesus Christ throughout the weekend. I was astonished to hear these words. I asked her how she felt this presence when I had not once mentioned the name of Jesus Christ. Her reply was clear, 'Yes, you did not mention him, and that is perhaps the reason why I felt it all the more in whatever you said and did. I felt that Jesus was present here among us; it was a wonderful experience, even to me; I'm not a Christian.' I replied that she could not make me a greater compliment and that I would keep what she said in my heart. I have been thinking about it repeatedly, and this experience has convinced me of the 'Way' Christ is in the spiritual journey that is sadhana.

On another occasion, the theme of my sadhana was explicit: Jesus Christ, Alpha and Omega, the Mystery of AUM. There too, most of the participants were not churchgoers. The experience, however, was highly rewarding. Several came to me and said: 'If that is Jesus Christ, I would be very happy to be his disciple and to live with him.' I had not spoken explicitly much about Jesus Christ. But a meditation of Father de Mello, the healing of the blind at the lake of Bethesda (John 5, 2-9) (*Contact with God*, 173-175) for example, had somehow deeply moved the sadhana participants. Today in the West, Jesus Christ is probably better preached in the silent testimony of life than in a wordy proclamation or sentimental outburst of 'Praised be Jesus Christ'. The picture that we Christians have diffused of him is just not appetising to the masses of the West. The Life-force of Jesus Christ does not pass through the age old theological signs and symbols. We need today to show the presence of Christ amidst life, where life takes place and unfolds.

As a matter of fact, several people who came to Father de Mello were somewhat dismayed to be exposed to more of psychology than prayer and spirituality. But their apprehension was quickly cleared when they learned to get in contact with themselves and with the flow of life in them. The living Christ is not a mere verbal proclamation. It is the expression of faith, that is, what bursts forth from the roots of one's being.

My own experience in Europe during the last thirty years is that many of the Europeans who call themselves Christians do not have deep roots in any form of Christianity. Often a deep resentment towards Christian discourse is to be noticed in them. However, these very people seem to be ready to accept Father de Mello's approach to the Christian message and, through it, come to discover their Christian roots. Through an over-development of theologising and conceptualising over the centuries in Europe, to the detriment of mystical experience, the Christianity that has been handed over from generation to generation now seems to take the form of a set of labels: a catechism of knowledge and not the art of kindling fire for discovering and experiencing God. Father de Mello tries to go beyond these labels. To use his own expression, he does not remain content to contemplate a bottle of wine and its label. Rather, he pulls out the cork in order to share the precious liquid with one and all and taste it. To this end, he finds effective methods from inside as well as from outside Christianity and his religious family of the Jesuits. He experiments with other spiritual traditions and the techniques developed in them. He brings them into his Christian experience, if that can be done without doing harm to either Christianity or the religions from which he borrows.

Father de Mello avoids traditional theological language. Theological terms like 'revelation,' 'salvation' and others are used by him more in their general sense accessible to the comprehension of modern man than in their technically theological sense. Furthermore, he does not try to identify spiritual experiences of other religions with Christian theological terms. For example, the state of liberty is not identified with 'salvation'. He keeps away from theological concepts and definitions for the simple fact that they provoke unending discussions over the terms and forms instead to going straight to their content. It becomes evident to his readers that his spirituality is imbued with clear intercultural and inter-religious traits. There lies, doubtlessly, an effort to point out the spiritual richness of humanity when experiences are made accessible to one and all instead of trying to contain them within fixed barriers of a given community.

Anthony de Mello was not particularly interested in so-called 'inter-religious dialogue', in which an effort is made to bring religions together in mutual understanding. Although inter-religious dialogue was quite popular during his lifetime, particularly after Vatican II, he did not play an active role in it. His interest was to experiment and discern that which was good and true in all spiritualities and traditions. Indirectly, that was probably the wisest approach, even for inter-religious dialogue.

A certain growth in this multi-spiritual dimension is clearly visible in his writings. His last works, particularly *One Minute Wisdom* and *One Minute Nonsense* are a synthesis of wisdom, good and wholesome for all human beings, brought out by the 'master'. What this master teaches is not just the spirituality of one particular tradition but a wholesome wisdom that has something positive and good to offer to all men. The wisdom of the Hindu-masters, the Zen-roshis, Taoist priest and monks, Jewish Rabbis, Christian monks and Sufi mystics meet to help to liberate man, from whatever walk of life or culture or religion, from his inner fetters. However, it should be noted that this inter-religious approach was not a new way of thinking that caught hold of de Mello. It was rather a sprouting forth of the seeds that were already there in his early works, even as he taught the *Spiritual Exercises* and wrote retreats.

Such an inter-religious synthesis might appear to some as a sort of a spiritual amalgam. Even some de Mello's supporters have occasionally, directly or indirectly, alluded to his supposedly post-modern intercultural spiritual mentality, accusing him of syncretism. Others have tried to classify him among the New Age writers, as it is often done by booksellers who place de Mello's books in their shops on the 'New Age' shelf. Further, the lightly humorous titles that de Mello gave to his books, *One Minute Wisdom* or *One Minute Nonsense*, for example, confirm the opinion of those who would like to see him classified as a New Age writer.

Anthony de Mello is certainly not a New Age writer, nor has he anything in common with it. Although what goes by the name of New Age has many positive aspects, it has the weak point of not respecting the respective profiles of cultures or religions from which it borrows. It is selective in its choices and picks up to suit its own preconceived ideas and network of values, leaving aside all other values cherished by those religions. The New Age person has no allegiance to any one religion he considers his own, but fabricates that which suits him best with numerous elements taken from different spiritualities. There is absolutely nothing of this idea in de Mello, who remains firmly in his Christian Catholic conviction and tries to understand and experience it in its depth with the help of all human beings, all cultures and religions. That is a different thing altogether. His Catholicity is not that of the so-called fundamentalists or traditionalists. He thinks with the church, the church of Vatican II.

As I have pointed out in his brief biography, his audience was essentially made up of religious people. Undoubtedly, the post-Vatican II spirit had brought about post-modern attitudes among the Jesuits and other religious people of Anthony de Mello's audience. He did not belittle or brush aside this mentality, but took it very seriously with great delicacy and attention, trying at every opportunity to lead people to a healthy spirituality. In his teachings he never made cheap compromises of his positions, beliefs and values. In fact, he is often very critical of the easy attitudes of modern men, and this criticism is particularly brought out through his caustic stories. What he seeks in his spirituality is to bring the modern person, torn asunder by fear, doubt and suffering to a healthy spiritual integrity, which is unified in his existence.

CHAPTER THREE

Father Anthony de Mello's Spirituality against the background of the Vatican's Notification

The *Notification concerning the writings of Father Anthony de Mello, S.J.*, issued by Vatican's Congregation for the Doctrine of the Faith on 24 June 1998 is composed of two texts: the *Notification* and the somewhat longer *Explanatory Note* which gives citations and references. Only the *Notification* is signed by the Prefect of the Congregation, Cardinal Joseph Ratzinger, and its secretary, Tarcizio Bertone. Furthermore, it has received the Papal blessing: 'The sovereign Pontiff John Paul II, at the audience granted to the undersigned Cardinal Prefect, approved the present *Notification*, adopted in the ordinary session of this congregation and ordered its publication.' (*Acta Apostolicae Sedis*, vol XC, pp 834 -5)

Only the *Notification* has been published in Latin in the official *Acta Apostolicae Sedis*. The omission of the *Explanatory Note* there is somewhat puzzling. Does it mean that the Congregation for the Doctrine of Faith withdraws it or does not subscribe its official authority any more to this document? In any case, the *Notification* read without the *Explanatory Note* remains an unjustified and somewhat mysterious document to a reader familiar with Father de Mello's works. For my study, I have taken the English version of both parts from the Vatican web-site: http://www.vatican.va/ (The site gives only the Latin text of the *Notification*, without the *Explanatory Note*. The full text can be obtained at http://www.ewtn.com/ library/CURIA/ CDF DEMEL. HTM

The Vatican texts, in the form in which they are published, particularly the *Explanatory Note*, are not easily readable. Ideas, texts and comments overlap; no paragraphs are made nor a numbering system adopted. To facilitate the readers to follow the study in its analyses and comments, I present the two texts synoptically in parallel columns by classifying the themes with sub-headings and numeration.

1. Father Anthony de Mello and his works

NOTIFICATION

• The Indian jesuit priest, Father Anthony de Mello (1931-1987) is well known due to his numerous publications which, translated into various languages, have been widely circulated in many countries of the world, though not all of these texts were authorized by him for publication.

EXPLANATORY NOTE

• The writings of the Indian Jesuit priest, Father Anthony de Mello (1931-1987) have circulated extensively in many countries of the world and among people of widely different backgrounds.

The immense success of the writings of Father Anthony de Mello was unforeseen by his publishers. Xavier Rio del Dias, director of the Gujarat Sahitya Prakash, the official publisher of Father de Mello's works in India, states that the real success of de Mello's books is not in the original English but in the Spanish translations published in South America, where literally millions read and enjoy them. The English editions in India have seen ten printings on average. Other editions in English have also appeared in America and in England. His first book, *Sadhana – A Way to God*, has been translated in over forty-five languages. The French publishers, Desclée de Brouwer in Paris and Bellarmin in Montreal, have jointly published six editions totalling over 50,000 copies. According to these publishers, the phenomenal success is not created by the press or by controversies provoked over the writings but solely by word-of-mouth. The German publisher, Herder, has now published over twenty books of Father de Mello, some of which were published in the German translation before their original English appeared in India! The commercial success of these books is so great that the publishers have subsequently printed newer editions of the same matter presented in more modern form with different titles.

However, following Father de Mello's death in 1987, the success of his books has gone wild. Given the demand among readers for his books, some publisherss have published books under his name with matter that cannot be attributed to Father de Mello or that which is a pitiful distortion of his ideas. These publications were not only unauthorised but were simply not written by Father de Mello. Unknown authors have published manuscripts under De Mello's name, cooking up texts which are composed of notes taken down by them or others from Father de Mello's conferences or from his broadcast talks, and into these they have profusely injected their own ideas. Such works highly contrast with those published by Father de Mello himself, who took immense pains to read and reread the manuscripts before sending them to the press.

Two works wrongly attributed to Father de Mello
From the very beginning of this study, I would like to draw attention of the readers to two works which are falsely attributed to Father de Mello both by the publishers of those works and by the Vatican. In fact, the most objectionable points raised by the Congregation for the Doctrine of Faith stem from these two works: *La illuminacion es la Espiritualidad* and *Walking on Water*. Both the works are amply quoted in the *Notification* to furnish so-called arguments against Father de Mello.

For the first, *La Iluminacion*, the Notification gives reference to the Spanish review *Vida nueva*. Sensing the strange ideas proposed there, I wrote to the *Vida nueva* in Spain to obtain a copy of it, but I was told that this work has now been re-edited under another title with the name of the author who composed it, Maria Paz Marino Barros, *Anthony de Mello. Testigo de la Luz*, PPC, Editorial y Distribuidora, S.A., Madrid, 1998 (8.a edicion). I insisted on receiving the first edition entitled *La Iluminacion*, which is quoted in the *Notification* and attributed to Anthony de Mello. The publisher refused my request for the reason that the work is out of print. I asked for a photocopy, but I was told that the original printing was too poor to be photocopied. Facing such insurmountable difficulties, I wrote to Cardinal Ratzinger at the Vatican to send me a photocopy of the work. I took the occasion to inform the Cardinal of my present work, and proposed to show it to him before it went to the press if he so wished. I received a reply from his secretary, Mgr Tarcisio Bertone (who is also the signatory of the *Notification*) who, without acknowledging my letter to the Cardinal nor mentioning anything about the other points in the letter, sent me the reference to the work, which was published as an offset of an article that appeared in the review *Vida nueva*, no 1585 (13 de Julio 1987) p 41 (1317) under the title: *La illuminacion es la Espiritualidad. Curso completo de Autoliberación Interior*. A student of mine in Madrid, searched the libraries and, after weeks of laborious work, got hold of the revue and sent me a copy. It is an article of about forty pages, composed of notes and commentaries taken down during talks and conferences. The author, given as 'Anthony de Mello', brings in a lot of ideas full of fantasies and ruminations from different fields. My student and friend, Luis Rodrigues, gave me an understanding of the whole story: *La Iluminacion* was probably the work of Maria Paz Marino. *Vida nueva* apparently published it without mentioning her name but attributing it to Anthony de Mello. It was only later, when people discovered its abominable contents, that the true author reworked it and published it under her own name in another edition, which is very different from the first with totally different contents. The Vatican authors of the *Notification* have not gone into the story behind this work. They have not even taken pains to consult Paz Marino's second reworked edition for, evidently, the first edition provided them with more nefarious stuff than the second.

The second work, *Walking on Water*, published in the United States by the Crossroad Publishing Company of New York, is a translation done by Philipp Berryman of two works that first appeared in Portuguese: *Caminhar sobre as águas* and *Quebre o ídolo*, published in 1992 by Edições Loyola, São Paulo, Brazil. It is known that Father de Mello did not speak Portuguese. The Columba Press edition, published outside the United States, clearly states that the text is based on retreats given by Fr de Mello in the USA and edited by Gabriel Galache SJ. The whole style of this work and its contents seem very different from the recognised authentic works of Father de Mello. Moreover, the presentation is not in the style of Father de Mello. It is known that he paid a great deal of attention to presentation, and the one that is adopted in this work seems to be entirely different.

THE NOTIFICATION

The Society of Jesus issued a warning in March of 1997 about these falsely attributed works, a year before the appearance of the Roman *Notification*. The Roman Congregation makes a small note of acknowledgement of this letter in the French edition of the *Notification*. There is no mention to it made in the English edition.

Father Xavier Dias del Rio, Father de Mello's official publisher in India, says that only the following six works, which were published under Father de Mello's care at the Gujarat Sahitya Prakash in Anand (India), are authentic: (1) *Sadhana – A Way to God* (1978), (2) *The Song of the Bird* (1982), (3) *Wellsprings* (1984), (4) *One Minute Wisdom* (1985) and (5 & 6) The *Prayer of the Frog Vols 1* (1988) and *2* (1989). Two more works were published posthumously by the same publishing house since, according to him, these manuscripts were kept by de Mello and were ready for print: (7) *Contact with God* (1990), and (8) *One Minute Nonsense* (1992). Furthermore, the work (9) *Call to Love* (1991) was also published at the same house, the manuscript of which was prepared by a close Jesuit friend and student of Father de Mello, Joseph Mattam SJ, from texts written by de Mello himself.

Another work, entitled (10) *Awareness* (1990), has been published in America under de Mello's authorship by another close Jesuit friend of Father de Mello, J. Francis Stroud SJ. This work has been met with immense success. There seems to be no doubt as to its authenticity, which Stroud presents as 'A de Mello Spirituality Conference in His Own words ... through his written and recorded words' (cf title page). Every sentence reflects de Mello's style and spirit as in the previously-mentioned nine works. I have no doubt as to its authenticity. However, the authorship of all other books attributed to de Mello needs to be carefully studied and verified.*

---

* The references to Father de Mello's texts quoted in this study are from the following editions: *Sadhana – A Way to God*, Gujarat Sahitya Prakash, Anand, India, 1st Edition, 1978; *The Song of the Bird*, Gujarat Sahitya Prakash, Anand, India, 4th Edition 1983; *Wellsprings*, Gujarat Sahitya Prakash, Anand, India, 6th Edition 1986; *One Minute Wisdom*, Gujarat Sahitya Prakash, Anand, India, 4th Edition 1987; *The Prayer of the Frog*, Vol 1, Gujarat Sahitya Prakash, Anand, India, 1st Edition 1988; *The Prayer of the Frog*, Vol 2, Gujarat Sahitya Prakash, Anand, India, 1st Edition 1989; *Contact with God*, Gujarat Sahitya Prakash, Anand, India,

Father de Mello's works, some of which he presents to people of all faiths, were initially meant primarily for religious priests and nuns, with whom he talked most of the time. Those were the ideas he developed for people who had a normal theological and spiritual formation but some of whom were suffering from an overdose of ill-served Christian spirituality in religious communities. However, even these people could quickly see the therapeutic goal in de Mello's affirmations, even when they seemed not to be so 'Catholic'. They understood his deeper intention, which was to shake them out of their routine spiritual rut and to bring them to the source of life. De Mello did not normally speak to lay people except on a few occasions, which were, for the most part, during his American tours. Towards the end of his life, he manifested a strong desire to get out of this habitual religious audience and attend to the needs of the laity and non-religious people of the world. But, unfortunately, his life came to a premature end. His works today are read in 'widely different backgrounds' (cf *Explanatory Note*), which is the real problem, because people without a Christian background and, worse yet, those with an ill-disposed Christian background, read and misunderstand him or drag him into their own wishful interpretations, as I shall amply note in the following pages. Unfortunately, the Vatican authors are not free from such misinterpretations. They, too, often read him out-of-context and interpret his writings as taking positions that he would never have taken, loyal as he was throughout his life to Jesus Christ and to his church. His permanent and unconditional loyalty to his Order, the Society of Jesus, was, in fact, a concrete expression of his loyalty to the Roman Catholic Church.

The *Notification* rightly points out the immense success of Father de Mello's books but does not make a just and adequate evaluation of their positive contribution to Christian spirituality and pastoral aid offered to such a large readership in the world.

1st Edition 1990; *Call to Love*, Gujarat Sahitya Prakash, Anand, India, 2nd Edition 1991; *One Minute Nonsense*, Gujarat Sahitya Prakash, Anand, India, 2nd Edition 1992; *Awareness*, Doubleday, New York 1992; *Walking on Water*, Crossroad Publishing, New York 1998; Brys, Aurel, and Pulickal, Joseph, *We Heard the Bird Sing*, Gujarat Sahitya Prakash, Anand, India, 1995

It takes cognisance of the warning issued by the Superior General of the Jesuits over the books wrongly attributed to Father de Mello in a footnote but does not take it into consideration in its evaluation of Father de Mello and in its judgements against him. They seem to avoid the painstaking enquiry of discerning the authentic writings of Father de Mello. The arguments brought against him are, for the most part, culled from such falsely-attributed works. Furthermore, the *Notification* does admit the 'widely different backgrounds' in which his works are read. They are also misinterpreted against such backgrounds. The Notification fails to point out the real – and almost only – background in which de Mello spoke and wrote, that is, to Jesuits and other religious men and women of India who understood him in the right perspective. It fails to distinguish between the true meaning and intention of the writings of Father de Mello and the misuse of his books by others. Further, it reads and interprets Father de Mello in a theological context, which was not his.

2. The Positive Features of the Teaching of Father de Mello: Oriental Wisdom

NOTIFICATION	EXPLANATORY NOTE
• His works, which almost always take the form of brief stories, contain some valid elements of oriental wisdom. These can be helpful in achieving self-mastery, in breaking the bonds and feelings that keep us from being free, and in approaching with serenity the various vicissitudes of life.	• In these works, which often take the form of short anecdotes presented in an accessible and easy-to-read style, Father de Mello collected elements of eastern wisdom which can be helpful in achieving self-control, in breaking the attachments and affections that keep us from being truly free, in avoiding selfishness, in facing life's difficulties with serenity without letting ourselves be affected by the world around us, while at the same time being aware of its riches.

The allusions made to Anthony de Mello's so-called 'Oriental' or

'Eastern' wisdom beg further commentary. What exactly does the Roman warning understand by the term 'Oriental wisdom'? Is it the exotic and somewhat charming idea that some Western thinkers have of Eastern thought, which they often shelve by respectfully calling it 'wisdom'? Father de Mello's Oriental wisdom cannot be limited to a teaching meant 'to break the bonds and feelings, attachments and affections' or a doctrine 'to approach life with serenity in the various vicissitudes of life'. Father de Mello never taught people to take airs of a peaceful and unperturbed Buddha sunken into meditation. The Eastern wisdom of Father de Mello, on the contrary, consists, in fact, just in those elements that are either ignored or those that provoke major difficulties for the Roman *Notification*. It is, namely, the teaching on attachment and detachment; the total emptiness to which the human soul can reach through awareness and awakening; the direct experience of God and the goal of spirituality as liberation and happiness.

Father de Mello, although he calls himself once 'an Eastern' in an article published in the review *Concilium* quoted above, cannot really be classified under the category 'Oriental Wise Man,' for he was educated in a Western milieu, spoke English at home and probably knew English literature and Western history better than Indian literature and history. His later education in philosophy in Spain and theology in Pune (India) were rather Western in form, and especially his psychological formation in the United States. It is only later when he began to work in India that he felt the need of delving deeper into his Indian roots. This research was not an effort to compare Eastern wisdom with Western knowledge or to try to prove the superiority of the East over the West. His sole aim in digging deep into Eastern spirituality was to show that it could admirably complement Christian and Western approaches to life. De Mello was not embellishing the Christian tradition with some rare Oriental jewels. The Oriental wisdom he learned led him, in reality, to question some of the fundamental attitudes and outlooks of present day Christianity, both in India and in the West.

The Roman *Notification* makes an effort to positively assess Father de Mello's 'Oriental wisdom' before undertaking a list of warnings against his teachings. However, the positive assessment is just a superficial combing over of what it calls 'Oriental wisdom'. The major aspects Father de Mello borrowed from Oriental traditions are either ignored or not appreciated.

3. Within the Boundaries of Christian Spirituality

NOTIFICATION	EXPLANATORY NOTE
• Especially in his early writings, Father de Mello, while revealing the influence of Buddhist and Taoist spiritual currents, remained within the lines of Christian spirituality.	• It is important to indicate these positive features which can be found in many of Father de Mello's writings. • Particularly in the works dating from his early years as a retreat director, while revealing the influence of Buddhist and Taoist spiritual currents, Father de Mello remained in many respects within the boundaries of Christian spirituality.

Continuing on the subject of positive appraisal, the Roman document notes elements in Father de Mello's spirituality 'within the lines or boundaries of Christian spirituality'. The text, understandably, does not specify what exactly the boundaries of Christian spirituality are. The Catholic Church knows a variety of spiritualities. The spirituality offered in parishes is not the same as that which is practised in religious communities. For example, the Jesuits practise a spirituality which is substantially different from that of the Franciscans or the contemplatives like Carmelites, Dominicans or Benedictines. The Christian mystics bring in elements that are often inaccessible to lay Christians and sometimes ones that are even shocking to them. However, one can understand what the *Notification* wants to express: that there are clear limits to Christian spiritual practices that need to reflect the message of the gospel and not contradict it.

However, the application of clear criteria in Christian spiritual practices is not always easy. The history of Christian inculturation through the ages has been continuously borrowed from other religions and cultures, practices of which the gospels do not always speak and which are not exactly in line with it: for example, the practice of religious vows, the institution of the Cardinals, etc. The contemplatives' way of life in cloistered monasteries, the singing of the office, the liturgy, the ascetical practices, vows and so forth are not exactly in line with what Jesus taught. They have been adopted by the church because such practices do not contradict the message of Jesus.

We could recall here the letter that Cardinal Ratzinger sent out on 15 October 1989 to the bishops on the topic of Christian prayer: Letter of the Congregation for the Doctrine of the Faith on some aspects of Christian meditation, *Orationis formas*, AAS 82 [1990]. In it, he questions the practices introduced by certain Catholics in their spiritual life and prayer, practices coming from so-called 'Oriental religions'. The Cardinal does not clearly specify what these practices are but, in a footnote, it is mentioned rather vaguely:

> The expression 'eastern methods' is used to refer to methods which are inspired by Hinduism and Buddhism, such as 'Zen', 'Transcendental Meditation' or 'Yoga' ... (2, note 1)

In this letter, the Cardinal explains what he considers to be the essence of Christian prayer:

> If the prayer of a Christian has to be inserted in the Trinitarian movement of God, then its essential content must also necessarily be determined by the twofold direction of such movement. It is in the Holy Spirit that the Son comes into the world to reconcile it to the Father through his works and sufferings. On the other hand, in this same movement and in the very same Spirit, the Son Incarnate returns to the Father, fulfilling his will through his passion and resurrection. The 'Our Father', Jesus' own prayer, clearly indicates the unity of this movement ... (7)

It is evident to one and all that the Christian prayer cannot be exclusively reduced to this theology of prayer, which is certainly Christian and should be given the most important place in the Christian spiritual life. But the Christian tradition has evolved and taken up other forms of prayer in which the two-fold movement of which Cardinal Ratzinger speaks is not always immediately and clearly visible. They can certainly be seen in them if we patiently and meditatively analyse them, as the Cardinal does with the Our Father. In this context, one can note that Father Anthony de Mello's book, *Contact with God*, is a splendid example of the prayer methods cherished in Christianity through the centuries.

The *Notification*'s concept, 'within the boundaries', needs to be better specified. Christian spirituality, since its inception, and over the centuries, has taken different elements from other religions and spiritualities. Its growth has not come to an end, and thanks to its very nature, it continues to grow. The present day teachings of the church on inter-religious dialogue and on inculturation are, again, an honest invitation to promote this growth. The boundaries of Christian spirituality, therefore, cannot be too firmly determined or closed. As I will point out later, Father de Mello does not preach any ideas that go against the Christian message and Christian traditions. Thus, it is unfair to say that only in certain points he remains within the boundaries of the church. In my opinion, he has always respected the real spirit of the Christian message and has on no occasion questioned the Christian tradition, nor tried to combat or reject it.

4. Acceptable Teachings

NOTIFICATION

• In these books, he treats

– the different kinds of prayer: petition, intercession and praise,

– as well as contemplation of the mysteries of the life of Christ, etc.

EXPLANATORY NOTE

• He speaks of waiting in silence and prayer for the coming of the Spirit, pure gift of the Father (*Contact with God: Retreat Conferences*, 3-7).

– He gives a very good presentation of the prayer of Jesus and of the prayer that Jesus teaches us, taking the Our Father as his basis (ibid, 42-44).

– He also speaks of faith, repentance and contemplation of the mysteries of Christ's life according to the method of Saint Ignatius.

- In his work *Sadhana – A Way to God*, published for the first time in 1978, Jesus occupies a central place, particularly in the last part ('Devotion', 99-134).

- He speaks of the prayer of petition and intercession as taught by Jesus in the gospel, of the prayer of praise and of invocation of the name of Jesus.

- His book is dedicated to the Blessed Virgin Mary, a model of contemplation (ibid, 4-5).

What the Vatican *Notification* underlines as positive points in Father de Mello: the 'Prayer of Jesus,' the 'Our Father,' the 'Mysteries of Christ's life,' the 'Prayer of petition and intercession' and the 'Prayer of praise and of invocation,' presented in the first part of *Sadhana – A Way to God*, mark, in fact, the early phase of his work as a spiritual father. Without abandoning these forms of prayer, and not in any way belittling them, de Mello reveals a clear growth in later stages of his life when prayer leads him to higher mystical states. The following testimony aptly describes this growth:

And then in 1985 I went to do a long sadhana. What struck me was the great change that had manifested itself in Tony. He had become very much involved with everything that was real: he enjoyed a good joke and relished a good meal, and he laughed boisterously and enjoyed every minute thoroughly, spending time with people and nature. I felt Tony had become one with another world. Could one call it the world of the spirits?

My last meeting with Tony was on May 27, 1987, after he had just finished the prayer seminar at Pune. I could see the fatigue in his eyes and a certain amount of weariness in his whole demeanour. Yet, all through the seminar itself Tony was in his element, enjoying every minute.
(*We Heard the Bird Sing*, 61)

There was indeed a change in him. But this change was never in contradiction of what he taught earlier. He had grown in his own methods of prayer, fulfilling them and never suppressing them.

The *Notification* observes some important points concerning Father de Mello's spirituality, but its recognition is insufficient, as has already been pointed out in the previous section. It is not enough to note only a few elements that clearly correspond to the traditional teachings of the church, but the *Notification* needs to make an appraisal of all of his teachings and of the general good that Father de Mello has done through them for a vast number of people. Through his help, many have regained the Christian 'force of life'. Also, many began re-practising their faith, and such an appraisal is called for, particularly when the points raised by the *Notification* cast doubt not only on some of his teachings but on his personality as well.

5. Progressive distancing from the Christian faith

NOTIFICATION	EXPLANATORY NOTE
• But already in certain passages in these early works, and to a greater degree in his later publications, one notices a progressive distancing from the essential contents of the Christian faith.	• But already in this work he develops his theory of contemplation as awareness, which seems to be not lacking in ambiguity.

However, the major accusation against de Mello is that his spirituality shows a 'progressive distancing from the essential contents of the Christian faith'. The *Notification* wants to underline that de Mello was quite 'all right' at the beginning but, later on, deviated from the essentials of the Christian faith. There is, however, a certain contradiction when it says that in his first works there were already deviations: 'But already in certain passages in these early works, and to a great degree in his later publications, one notices a progressive distancing from the essential contents of Christian faith.' If, in fact, there was a distancing, it was already present in his first writings.

It is wrong to talk of 'a progressive distancing' in the teachings of Father de Mello. His writings do not really reflect this deviation, nor does he express anywhere a will to distance himself from the church, the church's teachings or from the essentials of

Christian faith. His sayings need to be placed in their proper context, for he often asked and responded to questions in a given context. He was a good Jesuit up until the end of his life, who respected his superiors and these, in turn, esteemed him. In addition, he was a good Catholic priest and a good spiritual Father to one and all, including to several bishops. And this till the very last day of his life. It is true that people noticed an enormous change in him, but nobody interpreted this change as a distancing from the church or a distancing from the essential teachings of the Christian faith. They understood the meaning of it as a growth – a deepening of Christian Faith. If there was a distancing, it was from the morose, routine and perfunctory traditions in the Catholic fold.

As I noted earlier in the biographical notes, the 'growth' element was a very essential element in Anthony de Mello's life. At no moment did he pause to put forth a fully-fledged spiritual teaching, complete and ready for use for future generations. Every moment of his life was a moment of growth. One notices in his writings how he progressively became more and more expressive and direct in his allocution and also in his approach to spiritual guidance, to the point where he was open even to the so-called shock therapy.

Growth is not a foreign element in the Catholic Church. Since the works of Cardinal John Henry Newman (1801-1890), the teachings of the church have made room for the development of Christian dogmas. The church teaches that even the essentials of the Christian faith develop through the ages, following the Spirit acting through faith in the people of God (*Sensus fidelium*) and through the preaching of doctrine (*Lumen Gentium* 12, *Dei Verbum* 8). Anthony de Mello's perception of spirituality and, to a certain extent, his perception of the Catholic faith itself, had undergone such a growth. What was the *sensus fidelium*? In his case, it was the entire church of India, other churches where he was known and, most assuredly, the big family of the Society of Jesus, where his teachings were not considered at any time as a separation from the essentials of the Christian faith. On the contrary, all Jesuits, including his enemies, saw in it a powerful invitation to achieve a deepening of their faith. In other words, he was understood and appreciated by his own.

The *Notification* interprets the spiritual growth of Father de Mello as a progressive distancing from the church. Father de Mello has absolutely not distanced himself from the church. His growth has brought a new language, new concepts and new approaches to spiritual life either unknown in the Christian tradition or a revival of some of the known methods. De Mello did not always speak the traditional church jargon, but this does not mean that he was distancing himself from the church. One should not forget that his main concern was to speak to modern man, and he has, in that way, succeeded in developing a modern language that the present-day world understands, which the church authorities, for their part, have great difficulty in finding and using in their writings.

The *Notification* then continues to point out several fields in which Father de Mello marks the so-called distancing from the essentials of the Catholic faith.

6. SILENCE AS THE GREAT REVELATION

NOTIFICATION
• In place of the revelation which has come in the person of Jesus Christ, he substitutes an intuition of God without form or image,

EXPLANATORY NOTE
• Already at the beginning of the book, the concept of Christian revelation is equated with that of Lao-tse, with a certain preference for the latter: 'Silence is the great revelation,' said Lao-tse. 'We are accustomed to think of Scripture as the revelation of God. And so it is. I want you now to discover the revelation that silence brings.' (9; cf ibid, 11).

'Silence is the great revelation' – these are the opening words of the very first exercise in *Sadhana – A Way to God*. The title of the exercise is 'The Riches of Silence,' in which Father de Mello wants the exercitant to discover silence and the riches that silence brings. Read the text in the original English:

'Silence is the great revelation,' said Lao-tse. We are accustomed to think of Scripture as the revelation of God. And so

> it is. I want you now to discover the revelation that silence brings. To take in the revelation that Scripture offers, you must expose yourself to Scripture. To take in the revelation that Silence offers, you must first attain silence. And this is not easy. Let us attempt to do this in our very first exercise. I want each of you to take a comfortable posture.
> Close your eyes ...
> (*Sadhana – A Way to God*, 9)

It should be noted in the first place that the word 'revelation,' as applied to the Scriptures does not have the identical meaning when used to describe silence. The English language makes use of this word metaphorically and somewhat loosely, as in the expression 'It's revelation to me.' One is not referring to the revelation of the Scriptures, but that something is new or something is learned with some astonishment. De Mello uses the word 'revelation' in the second sense in this case. This idea is clear in the same exercise a little further on, when he says:

> Even those wandering thoughts of yours are a great revelation, aren't they? The fact that your mind wanders, isn't that a revelation about yourself? It is not enough to know this. You must take time to experience this wandering mind. And the type of wandering it indulges in – how revealing that is too!
> (*Sadhana – A Way to God*, 10)

From the context, it is very clear that Father de Mello has absolutely no intention of equating the revelation of the Scriptures with the revelation that silence brings. He wants the exercitant to experience the power of silence in the inner spheres of consciousness. He does not in any way deny the meaning or the value of the revelation found in the Scripture when he clearly makes the difference between 'the revelation that Scripture offers' and 'the revelation that silence offers'. Moreover, de Mello does not formally discuss the term 'revelation,' nor has he the slightest intention of criticising or belittling it in any way. A play on words made in a solitary text is not a theological heresy.

Father de Mello's teaching on silence as revelation needs a comment. He introduces in this context, in fact, a concept and an experience that are almost unknown in the West and in

Christian spirituality. Absolute silence is a state of being or consciousness in which even thoughts are absent. For the Oriental spiritual masters, it is the absolutely necessary state of mind for beginning to experience that which is spiritual. As the author of Yoga-suutra says, 'yoga is citta-v.rtti-nirodha, 'the silencing of thoughts'. The Buddhists also give great importance to the state of *sunyataa* or 'the emptiness'. De Mello wants to introduce this important experience into Christian prayer. He wants the Christian to experience something that is absolutely important:

> And as your silence deepens you will experience change. And you will discover, to your delight, that revelation is not knowledge. Revelation is power; a mysterious power that brings transformation.
> (*Sadhana – A Way to God*, 11)

Could this be an invitation for all Christians to experience the power of revelation rather than reduce it to mere concepts and words, thereby replacing spirituality with theology? Silence is not an enemy of the Christian revelation. The Christian spirituality has also given it an important place and has seen its relevance to spiritual progress. However, it should be noted that the silence of which the Oriental master speaks is not merely the absence of words or the disappearance of thoughts themselves, but a state of mind filled with God, with wonder and consolation.

De Mello does not attempt to equate Christian revelation with that of Lao-tse, nor does he show any 'preference for the latter' as the *Explanatory Notes* says. Father de Mello has nowhere 'preferred' Lao-tse to the Sacred Scriptures.

The *Notification* does not seem to appreciate the term 'revelation' used metaphorically in English. What de Mello means by this word 'revelation' is the astonishment that one experiences in silence, which seems like a wonder, revelation. He has, therefore, absolutely no intention of contradicting the revelation in Jesus Christ. The *Notification* seems to simply pick out one text and turn it into a problem without trying to see all of the texts in which Father de Mello makes use of the word 'revelation'. It is very clear that, elsewhere, he speaks of the revelation of Jesus Christ and respects it for what it is.

ANTHONY DE MELLO

7. The Heart and the Void

NOTIFICATION
• to the point of speaking of God as a pure void.

EXPLANATORY NOTE
• In exercising an awareness of our bodily sensations, we are already communicating with God, a communication explained in these terms: 'Many mystics tell us that, in addition to the mind and heart with which we ordinarily communicate with God we are, all of us, endowed with a mystical mind and mystical heart, a faculty which makes it possible for us to know God directly, to grasp and intuit him in his very being, though in a dark manner ...' (ibid, 25).
• But this intuition, without images or form, is that of a void: 'But what do I gaze into when I gaze silently at God? An imageless, formless reality. A blank!' (ibid, 26).
• To communicate with the Infinite it is necessary 'to gaze at a blank'. And thus one arrives at 'the seemingly disconcerting conclusion that concentration on your breathing or your body sensations is very good contemplation in the strict sense of the word. (ibid, 29-30)

In his concluding remarks on the richness of silence, in the first part of *Sadhana – A Way to God* (24-31), Father de Mello discusses the question of awareness and contemplation in five meditative exercises. With delicacy and finesse, he tries to answer the objections raised by the exercitant that 'these awareness exercises, while they may help for relaxation, have nothing to do with contemplation in the way we Christians understand the Word, and most certainly are not prayers,' (*Sadhana*, 24), objections which are shared by the *Notification*. He does not 'substitute' in any manner the intuition of God without form or image to the Christian revelation, which has come to mankind by way of Jesus. On the contrary, his effort in these pages are to bring in some mystical elements in approaching Christian prayer, which can sometimes become too wordy and complicated in the life of religious people.

In his spiritual vocabulary, Father de Mello understands the word 'prayer' as 'communication with God that is carried on mainly through the use of words and images and thoughts' (*Sadhana*, 24-25), whereas 'contemplation' is 'communication with God that makes a minimal use of words, images and concepts or dispense with words, images and concepts altogether'. This is the sort of prayer which John of the Cross terms *Dark Night of the Senses*, just as another author, a mystic monk of the fourteenth century, describes it as the *Cloud of Unknowing* (*Sadhana*, 25). Father Anthony de Mello's work as a spiritual master was to give his Jesuit companions a taste of prayer and the joy of prayer, which he himself had experimented and experienced in his personal life through the mystical methods that he outlines in *Sadhana – A Way to God*. He wants, therefore, in no way to destroy traditional Christian prayer and the concept of God in forms and images, for he writes:

> If the explanation does not satisfy you or only creates problems for you, then I suggest that you put aside all I say about this matter, and practise these awareness exercises merely as a means for disposing yourself for prayer and contemplation: or just ignore these exercises altogether and move on to others in this book that are more to your taste.
> (*Sadhana – A Way to God*, 24)

Furthermore, he later adds the following:

> I would not have you abandon all your prayer (communication with God that involves the use of words, images and concepts) in favour of a pure contemplation. There is a time for meditation and prayer and there is a time for contemplation, just as there is a time for action and a time for contemplation. (*Sadhana – A Way to God*, 30)

The burden of this section of the book is to show the exercitant that the exercises of awareness can lead to a real communication with God. In this context, Father de Mello develops the idea of the 'mystical heart', which the *Explanatory Note* mentions in the passage above. He explains how this mystical heart is often covered with dross composed of one's innumerable thoughts, distractions and mental activities that stifle it and diminish its capacities. The way of purification consists in creating absolute silence within. It is only through this silence that the heart develops and regains its capacities. The most effective way to create this silence is precisely through the art of awareness.

On this point, the best of the Christian mystical traditions meets, in fact, the best of the Oriental spiritual teachings. The author of *The Cloud of Unknowing*, or John of the Cross, meeting Patanjali, the author of *Yoga-suutra*. The pure void is not the final end nor is it the final reality. It is the mystical stage and the dark night through which the soul passes to see the rays of the rising sun, the vision of God.

The conclusion at which the *Explanatory Note* arrives is as follows: 'And thus one arrives at the seemingly disconcerting conclusion that the concentration on your breathing or your body sensations is very good contemplation in the strict sense of the word' seems to be a bit too hasty if the word 'thus' is not preceded by all the explanations that de Mello presents with great care, finesse and clarity, and which the *Explanatory Note* apparently does not seem to notice or brushes aside as being worthless.

The *Notification* does not seem to understand or does not want to understand Father de Mello's methods of reviving the prayer life of his brethren. In particular, the mystical heart seems to be disagreeable to it. This inner faculty, exploring the mystical spheres by going beyond ideas and images, held in high esteem by mystics in the church, is rejected here. 'Gazing at blank' is also known in the Christian tradition, but Father de Mello seems to borrow the method more from Buddhism. By experimenting with it in his own circles, he has found the method to be effective in Christian prayer.

8. Awareness, Awakening and Holiness

NOTIFICATION

EXPLANATORY NOTE
• In his later works, he speaks of 'awakening', interior enlightenment or knowledge: 'How to wake up? How are we going to know we're asleep? The mystics, when they see what surrounds them, discover an extra joy flowing in the heart of things. With one voice they speak about this joy and love flowing everywhere ... How attain that? Through understanding. By being liberated from illusions and wrong ideas.' (*Walking on Water*, 77-78; cf *Call to Love*, 97). Interior enlightenment is the true revelation, far more important than the one which comes to us through Scripture: 'A Guru promised a scholar a revelation of greater consequence than anything contained in the scriptures ... When you have knowledge you use a torch to show the way. When you are enlightened you become a torch.' (*The Prayer of the Frog I*, 86-87).

• Holiness is not an achievement, it is a Grace. A Grace called Awareness, a grace called Looking, observing, understanding. If you would only switch on the light of awareness and observe yourself and everything around you throughout the day, if you would see yourself reflected in the mirror of awareness the way you

> see your face reflected in a looking glass ... and if you observed this reflection without any judgement or condemnation, you would experience all sorts of marvellous changes coming about in you.' (*Call to Love*, 96).

The *Explanatory Note* brings up two points, one on 'awakening' and the second on 'holiness through awareness', themes to which Father de Mello accorded great importance. The text says: 'In his later works, he speaks of awakening, interior enlightenment or knowledge.' This is not just in his later works. One already finds such ideas in his very first works, *Sadhana – A Way to God* and also in *The Song of the Bird*. In the former he devotes about 50 pages (9-56) to awareness and its spiritual value; in the latter, the first twenty stories are on awareness.

However, the quotation which the *Explanatory Note* picks out from *Walking on Water* (77-78), makes the issue somewhat confusing. As we have pointed out above, the authorship of this work cannot be attributed to Father Anthony de Mello. The *Notification* has picked up a weak and confusing passage (an identical passage is not to be found in *Call to Love*, 97) to make De Mello's teaching somewhat ridiculous. It is rather difficult to prove in words and texts the spiritual benefits of awareness. One has to practise it. And the testimonies of those who have practised it consistently are the real proofs. I know that this experience is something new for Christians, especially to the teachers at the Vatican. That awareness alone can produce sanctity, is shocking. But that is a long and constant teaching of the Eastern religions, which Father de Mello brings into Christian spirituality. It would be regretful to refuse it. There are centuries of spiritual experience behind it to attest to its validity.

But what is 'interior enlightenment'? Father de Mello probably borrows this idea from the Zen Buddhism and the experience of *satori*. The yogic experience of *samaadhi*, or the Buddhist concept of awakening *bodhi*, too are experiences akin to what the Christian masters call *consolation* or in its higher levels *ecstasy*. Father de Mello explains the meaning of awakening through a beautiful story in *The Song of the Bird*:

> When the Zen Master attained Enlightenment
> He wrote the following lines to celebrate it:
> 'Oh wondrous marvel:
> I chop wood!
> I draw water from the well!'
> For most people there is nothing to wonder at in such prosaic activities as drawing water from a well or chopping wood. After enlightenment nothing really changes. Everything remains the same. Only now your heart is full of wonder. The tree is still a tree; and people are just what they were before; and so are you; and life goes on no differently. You may be as moody or even-tempered, just as wise or foolish as before. There's one major difference: now you see all of these things with a different eye. You are more detached from it all. And your heart is full of wonder
> (*The Song of the Bird*, 18-19)

Is there enlightenment in the Christian spirituality? Do we find something equivalent there? What the Hindus call *samaadhi* or the Buddhists *bodhi* comes close to what the Christian mystics call a 'state of consolation'. Just as enlightenment is experienced in stages, so too consolation can be small or an experience in depth. There are ample examples in the gospels to illustrate this moment of grace, joy and wonder that invade the heart when God visits it through the power of His Spirit. Elisabeth and her cousin Mary glorifying God:

> When Elizabeth heard Mary's greeting, the baby leaped in her womb; and Elizabeth was filled with the Holy Spirit. And she cried out with a loud voice and said, 'Blessed are you among women, and blessed is the fruit of your womb! And how has it happened to me that the mother of my Lord would come to me? For behold, when the sound of your greeting reached my ears, the baby leaped in my womb for joy.'
>
> And Mary said: 'My soul exalts the Lord, and my spirit has rejoiced in God my Saviour.' (Luke 1:41-47)

It is like the Roman centurion who feels in the depth of his heart his own lowliness, when he exclaims: 'Lord, I am not worthy for you to come under my roof, but just say the word, and my servant will be healed.' (Mt 8:8) Or Zachaeus filled with generosity:

When Jesus came to the place, he looked up and said to him, 'Zaccheus, hurry and come down, for today I must stay at your house.' Zachaeus stopped and said to the Lord, 'Behold, Lord, half of my possessions I will give to the poor, and if I have defrauded anyone of anything, I will give back four times as much.' (Lk 19:5 and 8).

The conclusion at which the *Explanatory Note* arrives: 'interior enlightenment is the true revelation, far more important than one which comes to us through Scriptures', was an objection which was already thrown at him (cf p 97 above). Father de Mello never tried to prove the superiority of his methods to those of Christianity; that was not his way of life. The *Explanatory Note* in fact misquotes the story of *The Prayer of the Frog I*, 86-87, and draws a conclusion which is absolutely not intended by the story. The story in question is:

A Guru promised a scholar a revelation of greater consequence than anything contained in the scriptures.

When the scholar eagerly asked for it, the Guru said, 'Go out into the rain and raise your head and arms heavenward. That will bring you the first revelation.'

The next day the scholar came to report: 'I followed your advice and water flowed down my neck-And I felt like a perfect fool.'

'Well,' said the Guru, 'for the first day that's quite a revelation, isn't it?'

The poet Kabir says:
What good is it if the scholar pores over words and points of
this and that but his chest is not soaked dark with love?
What good is it if the ascetic clothes himself in saffron robes but is
colourless within?
What good is it if you scrub your ethical behaviour till it shines, but
there is no music inside?

Disciple: What's the difference between knowledge and enlightenment? Master: When you have knowledge you use a torch to show the way. When you are enlightened you become a torch.
(*The Prayer of the Frog I*, 86-87)

THE NOTIFICATION

I should remark here that Father de Mello is making a joke. And the Vatican scholars behave something like the scholar in the story. He has no intention of ridiculing Christianity or any Scriptures (note that it is the *Explanatory Note* that makes use of the capital S). He demonstrates just how revealing it would be to experience life in its freshness and to take it as a revelation instead of droning on a recitation of the Scriptures. The word, 'revelation' is also used in the same metaphorical sense as in the passage quoted above. The Roman authors are making a problem out of something that can be understood from a Christian point of view. Catholic faith does not reject spiritual experiences of Christians in their daily life (Example: Thérèse of Lisieux). Christian Scriptures are not like the Koran, the Eternal Book in the presence of God to which all life should conform in all details, literally and word for word. The Catholic understanding of Scriptures is that they are tools for life, advice given to live out one's life on earth and to come to know God. When one is face to face with God, one will not be carrying one's Bible.

However, it should be noted that Father de Mello does not relegate the experience of 'Awakening' to the final day. It is an experience to be made in the here and now of this life, that's to say, each day when God visits human beings in the moment of his grace. The *Explanatory Note* cites the following quotation of Father de Mello without adding any comments to it: 'Holiness is not an achievement, it is a grace ...' (*Call to Love* 96). I do not see just what exactly is the difficulty raised by the Roman text. I guess it casts doubt on the idea of awareness as that which is linked to holiness. The passage quoted needs to be put in the right context in the writings of Father de Mello. It is taken from the 31st meditation from the book *Call to Love*, a meditation on verse Matthew 24:44: 'Therefore you also must be ready; for the Son of Man is coming at an hour you do not expect.' Father de Mello comments on this verse as that of contemporary men and women in the quest of holiness:

> Sooner or later there arises in every human heart the desire for holiness, spirituality, God, call it what you will. People look for it in books, consult gurus and build for themselves an illusive concept of holiness and spirituality, yet spirituality and holiness are not acquired in this manner:

> They have never stopped to consider this simple fact. Their efforts are going to get them nowhere. Their efforts will only make things worse, as things become worse when you use fire to put out fire. Effort does not lead to growth; effort, whatever form it may take, whether it will be power or habit or a technique or a spiritual exercise, does not lead to change. At best it leads to repression and a covering over of the root disease.
> (*Call to Love*, 95-96)

The whole meditation points to the meaninglessness of effort in spirituality. This is a counsel which Father de Mello gives in the first place to his own Jesuit brethren, for whom the whole enterprise of prayer and meditation can sometimes become a tiresome effort: 'Effort may change the behaviour but it does not change the person.' (*Call to Love*, 96) And then comes the passage, 'Holiness is not an achievement etc.' as quoted in the *Explanatory Note*. It may be useful to read the sentences following the quotation: 'Only you will not be in control of those changes, or be able to plan them in advance or decide how and when they are to take place. It is this non-judgemental awareness alone that heals and changes and makes one grow, but in its own way and at its own time.' (*Call to Love*, 96)

'But isn't awareness itself an effort?' rightfully asks Father de Mello.

> Not, if you have tasted it even once. For, then you will understand that awareness is a delight, the delight of a little child moving out in wonder to discover the world. For even when awareness uncovers unpleasant things in you, it always brings liberation and joy. Then you will know that the unaware life is not worth living, it is too full of darkness and pain.' (*Call to Love*, 96)

And in what way is this awareness linked to holiness? Will awareness bring the holiness that one desires? To which Father de Mello gives a more qualified answer:

> Yes and no. The fact is, you will never know. For true holiness, the type that is not achieved through techniques and efforts and repression, true holiness is completely unconscious. You wouldn't have the slightest awareness of its

existence in you. Besides you will not care, for even the ambition to be holy will have dropped as you live from moment to moment a life made full and happy and transparent through awareness. It is enough for you to be watchful and awake. For in this state your eyes will see the Saviour. Nothing else, but absolutely nothing else. Not security, not love, not belonging, not beauty, not power, not holiness, nothing else will matter any more. (*Call to Love*, 97)

Christian holiness has often been presented as a heroic act, meaning to say, a life spent in countless efforts and sometimes in self-torture. In the opinion of Father de Mello and according to the teachings of several Eastern spiritualities, such an effort builds only the ego and not a transformation of the person. Effort and self-torture become the ends in life. There lies probably the difficulty in accepting the concept of awareness, which seems to be too easy to lead to holiness. But if it does lead the person to wonder and awakening, and if it creates in him the continual joy of thanksgiving, then isn't it holiness? A gift to which one awakens rather than the realisation of an achievement?

Finally, 'when you are enlightened you become a torch' can be rightly understood, if by that we mean, as does Father de Mello, that the person is now so imbued with the entire doctrine of the Revelation that every word and gesture of his brings light to those around him as the words of the Revelation do. The person so radiating the 'divine' light will not put on haughty airs, as if he were supplanting the Revelation, but feel himself only a pointer to God and to his Word.

The *Notification*'s arguments in the section above are based on works wrongly attributed to Father de Mello. The *Notification* does not manifest openness towards a method introduced by de Mello from other religions, the idea of 'awareness'. Its use in Christian prayer, as the experience of many who practise it shows, far from deviating from the Christian prayer, brings to it a newness and intensity. The *Notification*'s conclusions are somewhat hasty and mocking. With an open heart, one could have better interpreted and understood Father de Mello's approach towards prayer. And on the whole the *Notification* has difficulties in understanding and appreciating Father de Mello's humour, which it takes for literal truth.

ANTHONY DE MELLO

9. THE APPROACH OF THE NOTIFICATION

NOTIFICATION

EXPLANATORY NOTE

• In these later writings, Father de Mello had gradually arrived at concepts of God, revelation, Christ, the final destiny of the human person, etc, which cannot be reconciled with the doctrine of the Church.

• Since many of his books do not take the form of discursive teaching, but are collections of short tales which are often quite clever, the underlying ideas can easily pass unnoticed. This makes it necessary to call attention to certain aspects of his thought which, in different forms, appear in his work taken as a whole.

• We will use the author's own texts which, with their particular features, clearly demonstrate the underlying thinking.

As has been previously pointed out, Father de Mello was neither a theologian nor a writer on Christian themes, such as those enumerated by the *Notification*. If, indeed, he occasionally touched on theological themes, that was purely out of the pastoral and therapeutic need of his clients, who were mostly priests and nuns who were well-aware and well-formed in their Christian and theological education, but whose problems in life sprung from other causes. They always understood Father de Mello and were capable of situating his positions in the right perspective. No one at any time raised serious objections about his theological positions, except the occasional joke about Rome taking him to task. The text of the *Notification* in the section above is a sort of introduction, explaining the approach that the document takes to the supposedly erroneous teachings of Father de Mello concerning the Scriptures, religions, God, Jesus Christ, ethics, morality and the church.

Father de Mello spoke a lot but wrote less. He felt that the written word somehow did not really convey what he wanted to say. On the other hand, he loved to express his teachings, like the preacher of Galilee, in stories and parables. He felt that the spiritual ideas in question were conveyed well by stories because they did not reduce the metaphor to fixed mathematical or juridical dimensions. For his listeners, the stories evoked the unseen and the ever growing meaning of their content of metaphor. He collected stories from various sources and recounted them in his own words, making them precise and apt in underlining the teaching on which he wanted to focus.

In its approach, the *Notification* makes a considerable effort to prove, by all means, the danger involved in Father de Mello's teachings by picking out sentences here and there. It fails to distinguish the pastoral and therapeutical context of de Mello's teachings. It fails to note the real context in which he preached, that is, exclusively to the Jesuits and to other religious people belonging to different orders whose religious, spiritual and theological education permitted them to see that there was no deviation on the part of their master in what he said and did. They certainly remarked exaggerations, but they had their place in the pedagogical approach of Father de Mello. He never spoke to the so-called New Age groups of people, who today often read and misunderstand him. But they do so the same with the gospels of Jesus Christ.

The humorous and 'witty-wise' sayings of Father de Mello are classed here as 'quite clever' with 'underlying ideas', as though Father de Mello wantonly indulged in an unfair play against the church and its teachings. The *Notification*, however, confronts real difficulties in coming to an end of its arguments. In several places, it fails to point out a clear passage to prove its hypothesis against de Mello and, therefore, makes very general statements like 'certain aspects of his thought which, in different forms appear in his work taken as a whole'. In fact, there is a certain ill-will manifested against Father de Mello in jumping from 'certain passages' to his 'work as a whole' to positions unten-

ANTHONY DE MELLO

able to the church. The text purports to quote the author's own words. But, as we shall point out, many of these quotations are not really from Father de Mello himself; one would expect a more scholarly and fraternal approach from the most respectful organ of our Catholic Church.

10. PERSONAL NATURE OF GOD IGNORED

NOTIFICATION

• To see God it is enough to look directly at the world.

• Nothing can be said about God; the only knowing is unknowing. To pose the question of his existence is already nonsense.

EXPLANATORY NOTE

• On various occasions, Father de Mello makes statements about God which ignore his personal nature, if not explicitly denying it, and reduce God to a vague and omnipresent cosmic reality.

• According to the author, no one can help us find God just as no one can help a fish in the sea find the ocean. (cf *One Minute Wisdom*, 67; *Awareness*, 103)

• Similarly, God and each of us are neither one nor two, just as the sun and its light, the ocean and the wave, are neither one nor two. (cf *One Minute Wisdom*, 34)

• With even greater clarity the problem of a personal Deity is presented in these terms: 'Dag Hammarskjöld, the former UN Secretary-General, put it so beautifully: "God does not die on the day we cease to believe in a personal deity" ...' (126) The same idea is found in *La iluminación es la espiritualidad* (60).

'If God is love, then the distance between God and you is the exact distance between you and the awareness of yourself?' (*One Minute Nonsense*, 266).

It is not at all true that Father de Mello does not teach one to have a personal relationship with God. His teachings are in fact steeped with personal relationship with God as Living Person. The meeting with a personal God through the most intimate and personal relationship with Jesus Christ is de Mello's fundamental credo. His *Contact with God* presents different methods of prayer, all warm and personal approaches to God addressed as Person. The third part of his *Sadhana – A Way to God* is on 'Devotion', that is, as Teresa of Avila describes it, to 'See him looking at you', ways to come to the personal God. His posthumous work *A Call to Love* is a strong appeal to love, love God in following Jesus' teaching. In the 18th meditation, on the 'Qualities of Love', based on the verse John 15:12, 'This is my commandment, that you love one another as I have loved you' Father de Mello says:

> That is why we are exhorted to be like God, 'who makes his sun to shine on good and bad alike and makes his rain to fall on saints and sinners alike; so you must be all goodness as your heavenly Father is all goodness. (52)

If, on occasion, Father de Mello seems to write, particularly in his stories, of an impersonal nature of God, those passages are to clearly underline a point before his religious audience, mostly priests and nuns, habituated to an almost 'human' concept of God, fallen in the rut of a routine relationship with God, as to a man. It is to make them wake up to God who cannot be reduced to the size of man. But such passages are rather rare in his writings.

The incapacity on the part of the writers of the *Notification* to understand what Father de Mello wants to say is well-illustrated in their interpretation of the story, 'Little fish in the Ocean,' to which we have referred in the previous chapter. Let us read the story:

> 'Excuse me,' said one ocean fish to another,
> 'You are older and more experienced than I, and will proba-

bly be able to help me. Tell me: where can I find this thing they call the Ocean? I've been searching for it everywhere to no avail.'

'The Ocean,' said the older fish, 'is what you are swimming in now.'

'Oh this? But this is only water. What I'm searching for is the Ocean,' said the young fish, feeling quite disappointed as he swam away to search elsewhere.

He came to the Master dressed in sannyasi robes. And he spoke the language of the sannyasi: 'For years now I have been searching for God. I left home and have sought him everywhere that he is said to be: on moun-tain peaks, in the heart of the desert, in the silence of monasteries and in the slums of the poor.'

'Have you found him?' the Master asked.

'I should be a conceited, lying man were I to say Yes. No, I have not found him. Have you?'

What could the Master say to him? The evening sun was sending shafts of golden light into the room. Hundreds of sparrows were twittering merrily away on a nearby banyan tree. In the distance one could hear the sound of highway traffic. A mosquito droned close to the ear, warning that it was about to strike ... And yet this good man could sit there and say he had not found God, that he was still searching for him.

After a while he left the Master's room, disappointed. He went to search elsewhere.

(*The Song of the Bird*, 14-15)

The *Explanatory Note* rather naïvely concludes from this story that, according to Father de Mello, 'No one can help us find God.' The reader will notice that the story is absolutely not against teachers of the faith, who help one to find God. In fact, it defends them. The story is really about a 'hard-nut' seeker of truth who does not want to see God where he is to be discovered, but searches for him through his own preconceived ideas of him and, through them, his own expectations about him. The little fish is not really looking for the ocean, but its preconceived idea of an ocean. He refuses to see the ocean when the more experienced fish points it out to him. Later on, having taken the form of a human being, he would seek God. When the master points at him, the reaction of the man is 'That is mere life. What I seek is God.'

The second reference cited by the *Explanatory Note* (*Awareness* 103) is, in fact, a beautiful explanation of the above idea given by Father de Mello himself:

> I need to talk about words and concepts because I must explain to you why it is, when we look at a tree, we really don't see. We think we do, but we don't. When we look at a person, we really don't see that person, we only think we do. What we're seeing is something that we fixed in our mind. We get an impression and we hold on to that impression and we keep looking at a person through that impression. And we do this with almost everything. If you understand that, you will understand the loveliness and beauty of being aware of everything around you. Because reality is there; 'God', whatever that is, is there. It's all there. The poor little fish in the ocean says, 'Excuse me, I'm looking for the ocean. Can you tell me where I can find it?' Pathetic, isn't it? If we would just open our eyes and see, then we would understand.
> (*Awareness*, 103)

To understand the second accusation raised against de Mello over the relationship between God and humans as being 'neither one or two,' we need to refer to the Hindu master, Ramaanuja, who, reacting against the teachings of the great *advaita* ('non-duality') master, Sankara, brought in a 'qualified' (*vi si.s.tha*) relationship between God and humans. He taught that the whole creation is the body of God, that is, the form through which God manifests himself continuously. The example that he brings is the manifestation of the ocean through its waves. The waves are inseparable from the ocean, but they are distinct from it. They are not two realities, nor are they just one reality. 'They are neither one nor two,' would say Ramaanuja. The position appears pantheist to the Christian understanding. But in reality it is a finely distinguished position against the absolute monistic teaching of Sankara, placing a distinction between God and his creatures.

The idea here is that the relationship between God and humans cannot be expressed through mathematical concepts of 'one' or 'two'. That God is 'one' is not a mathematical concept but a metaphysical, transcendental concept, which does not necessarily presuppose 'two' or 'three'. In the Christian faith 'one' has not the meaning of a radical monotheism of Islam (Surah 112). 'Not one, not two' is a new but subtle category of Ramaanuja that de Mello employs to express the mystical relationship between God and the human person and the mystery of Incarnation, whereby God takes form in matter, the two natures distinct but not necessarily separate: they are not one, not two.

The so-called 'impersonal terms' are not radical negations of personality but terms inviting one to a mystical experience that goes above ideas that we make of God and of our relationships with him. They lead one from the seen to the unseen and to the perfection of that which one imperfectly experiences through personal relationships here on earth. The quotation given by the *Explanatory Note* needs to be read in its context in full:

Dag Hammarskjöld, the former UN Secretary-General, put it so beautifully: 'God does not die on the day we cease to believe in a personal deity. But we die on the day when our lives cease to be illumined by the steady radiance of wonder renewed daily, the source of which is beyond all reason.' We don't have to quarrel about a word, because 'God' is only a word, a concept. One never quarrels about reality; we only quarrel about opinions, about concepts, about judgements. Drop your concepts, drop your opinions, drop your prejudices, drop your judgements, and you will see that.

Quia de Deo scire non possumus quid sit, sed quid non sit, non possumus considerare de Deo, quamodo sit sed quamodo non sit. This is St. Thomas Aquinas' introduction to his whole *Summa Theologica*: 'Since we cannot know what God is, but only what God is not, we cannot consider how God is but only how he is not.' (*Awareness*, 126-127).

The *Explanatory Note* misinterprets Dag Hammarskjöld's words. Neither the former secretary of the United Nations, nor Anthony de Mello, teach that God is impersonal; they simply underline 'that God does not die on the day we cease to believe in a personal deity.' These authors were trying to uphold the experience of God against a 'Death of God' theology that was at vogue at a certain time two decades ago and which is now dead and gone. God, in their eyes, was greater than our personal expressions of him.

Could it be that 'God' becomes a wearisome idea for many people because one has turned him into a concept and not an experience?

The reference made to *La iluminación es la espiritualidad* will not be considered here for the reasons I have already given.

The text quoted in the *Explanatory Note* from *One Minute Nonsense* (page 266) should be read within the context of the story:

'What you need is awareness,' said the Master to the religious-minded disciple, 'awareness, awareness, awareness.'
'I know; so I seek to be aware of God's presence.'
'God-awareness is a fantasy, for you have no notion of what God is like.
Self-awareness is what you need.'
Later he said, 'If God is Love, then the distance between God and you is the exact distance between you and the awareness of yourself?'

Certainly such a teaching can present a problem to those who are used to a certain etiquette or concept 'God'. Some spiritual fathers and pious Christians will not be at ease to place 'self-awareness' before 'God-awareness'. But the difference is that the 'God' discovered in the depths of the Self is not a concept. The God of love is not a distant deity. There is no distance between him and the person experiencing him, just as there is no distance between fire and the molten iron rod. Our fear comes probably from the idea of experiencing God in this manner.

'To see God it is enough to look directly at the world' is certainly one of de Mello's teachings. But as has been pointed out above, this expression looks naïve and unfounded if it is cut out from its context where de Mello explains it at great length and with painstaking precision. If one looks at the world as it is, then certainly one will not fail to see God. But one looks at it, alas, through the prism of one's own concepts and expectations. One labels what one sees and then one remains contented solely with those labels.

Father de Mello's teaching is on the art of looking at that which is contemplation. One certainly looks at things, but one's look is conditioned and coloured through one's own eyes of attachment, of appropriation. The day when attachments fall, the day when one can look at things through the eyes of detachment, then one will see things as they truly are, that is, signs pointing to something great; something beyond one's conceptions. They will be indicators of God. If God has become man and has touched matter, then the whole material world is an indicator of God, if only one can see it through the eyes of faith. It is the teaching of Jesus himself when he said: 'He who has seen me has seen the Father' (John 14:9).

This idea is also forcefully presented in the Eastern religions, notably in Hinduism and Buddhism, through their concept of *maayaa*. Apparently the West has difficulties in assessing this category of thought, and people have often translated this word as *illusion*. Yes, it is 'illusion', but not necessarily always in a negative and pejorative sense. *Maayaa* is the might, power and strength of the Almighty, it is a sign of God's work. But its meaning is not in itself but in what it alludes to. When persons see only the pointer and stop short of seeing the reality that is pointed to, then they are in illusion, they are deluded. When I point out the moon, do not look at my finger. When I wear glasses, I must look through the glasses and not try to contemplate the glasses themselves. It would be a grotesque illusion if I believed that the city of Zürich is just this word composed of six letters. For the mystic, that is, one who sees the reality, everything in this world is indicative of God. It is enough to look at the world to see God.

We will treat the objection raised by the Roman letter: 'Nothing can be said about God, the only knowing is unknowing' under the 'radical apophaticism' which presently follows. However, 'God is considered as a cosmic reality, vague and omnipresent' are not Father de Mello's words. He has never spoken of God as a 'vague' thing. If he sometimes developed an apophatic language, it was not meant to develop an impersonal idea of God, but just the opposite: to shake up those who were, in their belief, a bit too habituated towards a God who is reduced to human dimensions.

The *Notification* and the *Explanatory Note* do not try to present de Mello's position by assessing his overall teachings. The Vatican authors seem to have first made up their mind to condemn him and then go 'fishing' for arguments to substantiate their condemnation by picking out texts here and there and by distorting them to suit their prejudices.

Furthermore, I do not see why the *Notification* finds fault with Father de Mello on the point of God being close to oneself in love. I read there the most fundamental Christian teaching on the incarnation of God, God become man, Emmanuel. The *Notification* does not adduce references to Father de Mello's writings to substantiate its objection: 'To pose the question of his existence is already nonsense.' I cannot find this text or one similar to it in Father de Mello's writings. It seems to me that the conclusion is simply a misunderstanding of Father de Mello.

11. THE RADICAL OR EXAGGERATED APOPHATISM

NOTIFICATION

- This radical apophaticism

EXPLANATORY NOTE

- Following from a unilateral and exaggerated apophaticism which is the consequence of the above-mentioned concept of God, criticism and frequent irony are directed toward any attempt at language of God.

- The relationship between God and creation is frequently expressed with the Hindu image of the dancer and dance: I see Jesus Christ and Judas, I see victims and persecutors, the killers and the crucified: one melody in the contrasting notes ... one dance moving through different steps ... Finally, I stand before the Lord. I see him as the Dancer and all of this maddening, senseless, exhilarating, agonizing, splendorous thing that we call life as his dance ... (*Wellsprings: A Book of Spiritual Exercises*, 200-201; *The Song of the Bird*, 16). Who or what is God and what are men in this 'dance'?

- And again: 'If you wish to see God, look attentively at creation. Don't reject it; don't reflect on it. Just look at it' (*The Song of the Bird*, 27).

- It is not at all clear how Christ's mediation for knowledge of the Father enters into such a description. 'Realizing that God has nothing to do with the idea I form of

> God ... There is only one way of knowing him: by unknowing!' (*Walking on Water*, 12; cf ibid, 13-14; *Awareness*, 123; *The Prayer of the Frog I*, 268).
>
> • Concerning God, therefore, one cannot say anything: 'The atheist makes the mistake of denying that of which nothing may be said ... And the theist makes the mistake of affirming it.' (*One Minute Nonsense*, 21; cf ibid, 336).

The term 'apophatism' (derived from Greek word, *apophemie*, which means 'I deny') refers in theology to the affirmation of God by way of negation. Being above everything created, no created intelligence can conceive God as he is and, consequently, no human language can express him adequately. There is no word, no symbol that can be an adequate description of God. Therefore, the most appropriate way to speak about him is through negative concepts, that is, to describe what God is not or place predicates empty of positive content: silence, void, vacuity, emptiness and so forth.

Since the very beginning of Christianity and of Christian theology this negative (*apophatic*) theology has coexisted with the affirmative (*kataphatic*) explanation of God. The early Fathers of the Church like Justin, around the year AD 150, taught that 'Nobody can give a name to the ineffable God.' (1 Apol 61, 110) The Fathers of the Church, taking over Greek traditions, adopted this way of speaking about God notably against paganism, which pictured God through polytheistic and anthropomorphic concepts. They were upholding the pure knowledge of God, particularly in the difficult task of explaining the divine nature of Jesus Christ.

Apophatism becomes a theology with Denys the Areopagite (c. 500 AD) who, taking up a number of new ideas, structured a theology to explain the transcendence of God through strong apophatic terms. His teachings are then taken up by all major theologians of the Middle Ages starting with Thomas Aquinas (1225-1274), Meister Johann Eckhart (1260-1328), John Ruysbroeck (1293-1381), Nicholas of Cusa (1401-1464) and others.

Father de Mello has a beautiful chapter on God in apophatic terms in his book, *Awareness*. He takes Thomas Aquinas as his major authority for this approach. He wonders how this great saint and doctor of the church, who wrote a great deal of theological treatises over difficult and different questions, fell silent towards the end of his life and refused to speak anymore and stopped writing. He had experienced something very profound. He had felt God and, in comparison with this experience of God, all that he wrote and discussed about him earlier appeared to him as worthless.

Even before this silence fell upon him, he had felt that the human knowledge of God would not lead him to his essence. He taught that we cannot say who God is; we can only say what he is not. The following are Father de Mello's thoughts on Thomas Aquinas:

> In the prologue of his *Summa Theologica*, which was the summary of all his theology, he (Thomas Aquinas) says, 'About God, we cannot say what he is but rather what he is not. And so we cannot speak about how he is but rather how he is not.' And in his famous commentary on Boethius' *De Sancta Trinitate* he says there are three ways of knowing God: (1) in the creation, (2) in God's actions through history, and (3) in the highest form of the knowledge of God – to know God *tamquam ignotum* (to know God as the unknown). The highest form of talking about the Trinity is to know that one does not know. Now, this is not an Oriental Zen master speaking. This is a canonised saint of the Roman Catholic Church, the prince of theologians for centuries. To know God as unknown. In another place St Thomas even says: as unknowable. Reality, God, divinity, truth, love are unknowable; that means they cannot be comprehended by the thinking mind. That would set at rest so many questions people have because we are always living under the illusion that we know. We don't. We cannot know.
> (*Awareness* 100)

THE NOTIFICATION

The *Notification* coins an expression 'radical apophatism' which is not to be found in the vocabulary of the apophatic tradition of the Catholic theology. 'Apophatic' means 'negative' and, therefore, it is difficult to speak of an *absolute* negativity or to qualify it by *radical* or *unilateral* apophatism. Something is either negative or it is not.

However, one can understand what the *Notification* wants to express by this term 'radical apophatism.' It probably refers to some of the teachers in this tradition who upheld only a negative discourse on God, excluding all affirmative ideas about him. It seems to follow the thinking of some church theologians who doubted the validity of an apophatic theology on account of the danger of atheism, or promotion of a certain attitude of irresponsibility for human action. The language of the gospels is positive and not apophatic; so also is the tradition of the church in general which expresses itself in an affirmative theology. For example, God is a positive concept: the Father, the Creator, the Judge, the Redeemer and so forth. It is he who has manifested himself concretely in time and space through his Son, Jesus Christ. The *Notification* probably reacts also to the present day influence of Buddhism in the West, whose concept of *nirvana* is an apophatic concept excluding all positive ways of thinking of reality. The church has difficulty in appreciating the fascination shown to it more and more by present-day Westerners since Schopenhauer and Nietzsche.

But let us be clear on this point: Father de Mello in no way promotes such a radical apophatism. For, first of all, like all the apophatic theologians in the past who developed their teaching in a particular context, Father de Mello too has a very clear context for his apophatic teaching. He writes, 'The fanaticism of one sincere believer who thinks he knows, causes more evil than the united efforts of two hundred rogues. It's terrifying to see what sincere believers will do because they think they know.' (*Awareness*, 101) Let us not forget that the young Tony belonged to this type of Christian who went by the certitude of their knowledge of Christian faith and dogmas. The problem with such certitude is that in the long run it does not give force to life. It does not give birth to a faith which diffuses strength. They grow up to be human efforts to stifle the word of God through the bounds of human knowledge. This tendency is evident in certain circles of theology which are more concerned with theological precision of words rather than with their content. We notice it again in some of our church teachers who preach a message of this lifeless certitude. As de Mello explains, 'Wouldn't it be wonderful if we had a world where everybody said: "We don't know?" One big barrier dropped, wouldn't that be marvellous?' (*Awareness*, 101)

As I said earlier, the pernicious tendency in theology is to reduce God to a mere concept. One holds on to this concept and somehow glorifies and adores it instead of appreciating its content. One can recall Tony's words: 'No one ever became drunk on an intellectual understanding of the word *wine*' (*Song of the Bird*, 3). He explains further:

> A man born blind comes to me and asks, 'What is this thing called green?' How does one describe the colour green to someone who was born blind? One uses analogies. So I say, 'The colour green is something like soft music.' 'Oh,' he says, 'like soft music.' 'Yes,' I say, 'soothing and soft music.' So a second blind man comes to me and asks, 'What is the colour green?' I tell him it's something like soft satin, very soft and soothing to the touch. So the next day I notice that the two blind men are bashing each other over the head with bottles. One is saying, 'It's soft like music'; the other is saying, 'It's soft like satin.' And on it goes. Neither of them knows what they're talking about, because if they did, they'd shut up. It's as bad as that. It's even worse, because one day, say, you give sight to this blind man, and he's sitting there in the garden and he's looking all around him, and you say to him, 'Well, now you know what the colour green is.' And he answers, 'That's true. I heard some of it this morning!
>
> The final barrier to the vision of God is your God concept. You miss God, because you think you know. That's the terrible thing about religion. That's what the gospels were saying, that religious people knew, so they got rid of Jesus. The highest knowledge of God is to know God as unknowable. There is far too much God talk: the world is sick of it. There is too little awareness, too little love, too little happiness, but let's not use these words either. There is too little dropping of

illusions, dropping of errors, dropping of attachments and cruelty, too little awareness.' (*Awareness*, 101-102)

When one looks at the present-day situation of religions, one notices often how the knowledge of God provokes war rather than peace. God cannot be preached in such a way as to make of him a source of hate, violence and destruction. The richness of the religious experience also shows how those who were imbued by God never provoked hate, violence and destruction. The context in which Father de Mello develops his apophatic language is precisely our modern world in which many men and women are scandalised by what religions make of their God. The 'God-talk' that one hears here so frequently from pulpits and from learned texts is so far removed from the reality of today's world that it not only appears to them as impertinent but also scandalous when followers of one religion are barred from the other just because of their concept of God. Father de Mello cites the following example:

> The great Karl Rahner, in one of his last letters, wrote to a young German drug addict who had asked him for help. The addict had said, 'You theologians talk about God, but how could this God be relevant in my life? How could this God get me off drugs?' Rahner said to him, 'I must confess to you in all honesty that for me God is and has always been absolute mystery. I do not understand what God is; no one can. We have intimations, inklings; we make faltering, inadequate attempts to put mystery into words. But there is no word for it, no sentence for it.' And talking to a group of theologians in London, Rahner said, 'The task of the theologian is to explain everything through God, and to explain God as unexplainable.' Unexplainable mystery. One does not know, one cannot say. One says, 'Ah, ah ...' (*Awareness*, 124).

This exclamation is a reference to the Hindu text *Kena-Upani.sad*, which says that the symbol of Aatman (the highest indwelling Reality) is 'Ah, ah' that one utters when a fissure of lightning appears in the sky (*Kena-upani.sad* IV,4)

Talking about God in absolute, exaggerated and unilateral certitudes can bring forth an idolatrous attitude. This context is the one that Father de Mello particularly has in his mind in his use of the apophatic language:

> Tragically, people fall into idolatry because they think that where God is concerned, the word is the thing. How could you get so crazy? Can you be crazier than that? Even where human beings are concerned, or trees and leaves and animals, the word is not the thing. And you would say that, where God is concerned, the word is one thing? What are you talking about? An internationally famous scripture scholar attended this course in San Francisco, and he said to me, 'My God, after listening to you, I understand that I've been an idol worshipper all my life!' He said this openly. 'It never struck me that I had been an idol worshipper. My idol was not made of wood or metal; it was a mental idol.' These are the more dangerous idol worshippers. They use a very subtle substance, the mind, to produce their God.
> (*Awareness*, 124-125)

Furthermore, when Father de Mello teaches that nothing can be said about God and that the only knowing is unknowing, one must remember that these words were written or pronounced in a pastoral context. It was not the dogmatic context in which the church taught about the knowledge of God, the natural knowledge whereby an intellect is capable of recognising God's existence. When the church teaches that one can know God in spite of the fact that God is a mystery, it teaches in reality that the human being is not at a loss before God, even when faith has not yet dawned in one's heart. In one's very being and essence, the human being is made for God and so the concept of God is not a contradiction to one's intelligence.

There is certainly no place in Christianity for an exclusive apophatic theology. But a sound apophatic approach can complete and correct a radical affirmative theology. A pure apophatic language does not bring out the 'flesh and blood,' which is essential to the Catholic Church. Father de Mello's apophatic teachings have only a very small place in his vast writings and discourses which are full of positive formulation of God, a spirituality, deeply personal and person-centred in the spirit of Ignatius of Loyola. It is unjust to accuse him of radical apophatism when most of his writings on prayer and the mystical experience of God are written in affirmative language, that's to say, underlining the feel and taste of God through concrete awareness of this life and existence. The authors of the *Notification* could have profitably read another passage of Father de Mello in the same chapter as quoted above:

> How sad if we pass through life and never see it with the eyes of a child. This doesn't mean you should drop your concepts totally; they're very precious. Though we begin without them, concepts have a very positive function. Thanks to them we develop our intelligence. We're invited, not to become children, but to become like children. We do have to fall from a stage of innocence and be thrown out of paradise; we do have to develop an 'I' and a 'me' through these concepts. But then we need to return to paradise. We need to be redeemed again. We need to put off the old man, the old nature, the conditioned self, and return to the state of the child but without being a child. When we start off in life, we look at reality with wonder, but it isn't the intelligent wonder of the mystics; it's the formless wonder of the child. Then wonder dies and is replaced by boredom, as we develop language and words and concepts. Then hopefully, if we're lucky, we'll return to wonder again.
> (*Awareness*, 126)

The author used to employ such an expression in Jesuit communities against exaggerated stereotypes and routine in mechanical recitation of prayer and celebrations. Of course, this style outside strict religious circles can appear, as it does, to be both critical and ironic. However, irony for the sake of irony and sarcasm to belittle others was totally absent in Father de Mello. His Jesuit and other religious audience did not fail to 'catch his drift' and join him in a boisterous laugh.

The *Explanatory Note* quotes a metaphor which Father de Mello loved to repeat in his talks and writings, that of 'the dancer and the dance', the Hindu concept of God being the dancer and the creation being his dance. The metaphor needs to be read in its entirety as narrated by Father de Mello:

> Hindu India developed a lovely image to describe the relationship between God and his Creation. God 'dances' his

Creation. He is the Dancer, his Creation is the Dance. The dance is different from the dancer; and yet it has no existence apart from him. You cannot take it home with you in a box, if it pleases you. The moment the dancer stops, the dance ceases to exist.

In his quest for God, man thinks too much, reflects too much, talks too much. Even when he looks at this dance that we call creation, he is the whole time thinking, talking (to himself and others), reflecting, analysing, philosophising. Words, words, words. Noise, noise, noise.

Be silent and look at the dance. Just look: a star, a flower, a fading leaf, a bird, a stone … Any fragment of the Dance will do. Look. Listen. Smell. Touch. Taste. And, hopefully, it won't be long before you see him – the Dancer himself!

(*The Song of the Bird*, 16)

The Hindu image is full of mystery and awe. It is the Dance of the great God Shiva, the Tandava Dance that is, the dance of the Creation and Destruction of the universe. Marking the two phases of the cosmic cycle, the evolution and the involution, the Creator 'dances out' the Creation and reabsorbs it. God creates and destroys, not because he has any desire to fulfil in those acts. He acts out of his purest joy (*aananda*) which is his essence. It is God's play (*liilaa*), ignorance (*avidyaa*) to the human being. The Hindu remains in awe before this mystery (*maayaa*) of Creation. The immense cosmic dance, which comes into being out of the rhythm struck by Shiva's feet and his movements, is unseen by the creatures who are but small particles in this gorgeous cosmic panorama. They are not placed so as to get a full picture of the dance. Instead of trying to identify the Dancer, they let themselves be taken up by transitory details, which they take to be absolute and find their contentment in them. That is the ignorance (*avidyaa*) of the creatures, which has to be overcome so that one comes to see the totality of the dance and, above all, the Dancer himself. How does one recognise the Dancer? Not through the unending 'talk,' that's to say, mental and rational investigations, but in the silent, wordless contemplation of the dance: '… it won't be long before you see him – the Dancer himself!' This cosmic dance evokes a mystical meditation which the Roman writers unfortunately fail to appreciate. They instead raise the following doubt: 'Who or what is God and what are men in this 'dance'?' Again, the metaphor is used to explain that we come to God through his creation. It is not a dogmatic discourse on God and men. This Hindu imagery, which might appear as atrociously pagan to a Roman mind, is not incompatible with the Christian notion of God. But the Christian concept of incarnation is just this view, as attested by the liturgy of Christmas:

In the wonder of the Incarnation
your eternal Word has brought to the eyes of faith
a new and radiant vision of your glory.
In him we see our God made visible
and so are caught up in love of the God we cannot see.
(Preface, Midnight Mass)

The Christian teaching of the providence of God is again a further consequence of the mystery of God become man. As Paul addresses the Athenians: 'For in him we live, and move, and have our being; as certain also of your own poets have said, For we are also his offspring.'(Acts 17:28) And this assurance is given not only to the just and the pure but also to the unjust and the sinful, who are all upheld in life by God through his loving providence. So the statement 'this maddening, senseless, exhilarating, agonising and splendid thing that we call life is his Dance' belongs to the loving providence of God.

The *Explanatory Note* then makes a remark on Christ's mediation, which we can take up now, although a separate section will be devoted to the christological problems. It is the fundamental Christian teaching that Jesus Christ is the Son of God and that all God's action with humanity takes place in and through Jesus Christ. Father de Mello casts no doubt over this teaching. The revelation of God in and through Jesus Christ, 'He who has seen me has seen the Father' (John 14:9), is not contradicted by the metaphor of Dance. The whole creation is Christic. But Christ in his personal – but also in his cosmic- dimensions is not identical with God. He is full (*totus*) God, but not entirely (*totum*) God. The human reality and the human eyes do not allow us to capture the entire God-vision in Jesus Christ. Secondly, it might be useful to note that Father de Mello does not write a christological treatise on the mediation of Christ but a poetical metaphor to emphasise a spiritual point, that is, the mystical experience of God through the creation.

Father de Mello's concept of God and of the experience of God is deeply influenced by the teachings of St Ignatius of Loyola, the founder of his religious order. This spiritual master did not teach his disciples a particular christology, that is, a particular theological discourse on Christ, but a simple and direct experience of God through Jesus Christ. He spoke of touching God, feeling God, experiencing God. He loved the old prayer full of piety: *Soul of Christ sanctify me; Body of Christ save me; Blood of Christ inebriate me*, a leitmotiv in his *Spiritual Exercises*. He taught his companions to love God directly and intimately through the Flesh and Blood of Jesus. It is this experience of God that Father de Mello constantly teaches and brings to his students' attention, through direct and positive terms. Every meditation and every conference is filled with this idea of God. I am astonished at the attitude of the *Notification* which makes a problem out of de Mello's rare apophatic thoughts by closing their eyes to his positive teachings on God.

For Father de Mello, prayer was a profound relationship with the personal God. To bring out the deeper strains of this relationship in prayer, he took ideas and symbols from other religions and other cultures. The following Hindu school of loving devotion (*bhakti*) is a good example:

> Lord, I ask you to pardon me for three major sins: first, I went on pilgrimage to your many shrines, oblivious of your presence everywhere; second, I so often cried to you for help, forgetting that you are more concerned than I about my welfare; and finally, here I am asking for forgiveness when I know that our sins are forgiven before we commit them.
>
> (*The Prayer of the Frog I*, 6)

Contemplating God in all things, meeting him and feeling his love in all deeds, is the crowning goal of the *Spiritual Exercises* of Ignatius of Loyola. A Jesuit is trained from his early noviciate to deeply enter into a personal relationship with God, to contemplate and to taste God in all details of life by trying to live in perfect obedience to his will. Anthony de Mello made it the central theme of his spirituality. And he never deviated from it. He writes that:

> One needs to do so little, really, to experience God. All one needs to do is quieten oneself, become still – and become aware of the feel of your hand. Be aware of the sensations in your hand ... there you have God, living and working in you, touching you, intensely near you ... Feel him. Experience him!
>
> We forget all too easily that one of the big lessons of the incarnation is that God is found in the ordinary. You wish to see God? Look at the face of the man next to you. You want to hear him? Listen to the cry of a baby, the loud laughter at a party, the wind rustling in the trees. You want to feel him? Stretch your hand out and hold someone. Or touch the chair you are sitting on or this book that you are reading. Or just quieten yourself, become aware of the sensations in your body, sense his almighty power at work in you and feel how near he is to you. Emmanuel. God with us.
>
> (*Sadhana – A Way to God*, 42)

Spirituality is precisely this centring of life on God. Only a deep personal relationship can create such a centring. In one of his exercises, Father de Mello teaches the concept concretely. He asks the exercitant to make a list of his desires: the great desires, the small ones, the 'romantic' desires, the prosaic ones and so forth. Similarly, he asks him to make a list of some problems with which one grapples in life: family problems, job problems, personality problems. Then he comes to topic of the contact with the personal God and asks himself, 'What part am I giving to God in the fulfilment of these desires of mine?'

> Does he play a role in making these desires come true? What role? Am I satisfied with the role he has? Is he?
>
> Then ask yourself: What part am I giving to God in the solution of the problems that I am dealing with currently? ... How much am I relying on him in solving them? ... How much trust do I have in him? ...
>
> (*Sadhana – A Way to God*, 129-130)

More questions are raised then to strike deeper relationships with God: Where does God feature in my list of desires? Where does God feature in my list of problems? Father de Mello then asks the exercitant to consciously observe in fantasy how he or she attempts to realise them:

Now expose every one of these means to God and to his influence ... What is important here is exposure, not results ... See every action, thought etc as coming from God and moving towards God ...'
(Sadhana – A Way to God, 129-130)

Such a spiritual counselling was, in fact, often a therapy or a healing offered to religious men and women who came to him with sad experiences of a 'tyrannical God' who was imposed on them even from their early childhood. One of de Mello's disciples testifies by reproducing moments of a spiritual counselling session:

Sebastian: I have a great fear of God: when I imagine God I feel low, thrown down, small. I do tell people of God's mercy and goodness, but I don't feel at all that way.
Tony: Who is frightening you?
S: God is, he keeps me down looking so piercingly.
T: Who is drawing that picture?
S: I.
T: Quite sure?
S: May be I got it from someone and I am putting it on God. Maybe he is that way.
T: Maybe he is that way!
S: Then I will be justified in my fear: yes, maybe he is that way or maybe I project that image onto him.
T: Are you comfortable with that ambivalence or are you frightened?
S: I am always in suspense about it.
T: What and who and how God, Ultimate Reality, is, I do not know: I make an act of trust and occasionally I experience him as merciful. Yes, it could ultimately prove to be a cruel joke, but that doesn't rub me, it rubs you. You want to stop letting it rub you?
S: I would like to, but I am afraid to let go, to take the step.
T: Here a strength is needed which you now use against yourself. Whenever you start nagging yourself, being frightened, you put your strength on him to put yourself down. Job fought him and in the end Job won. You are saying to yourself and you consider yourself worthless; and so many

teachers, retreats, religious sermons, etc ... keep you convinced of that.

'Fear of God': it is our own cruelty and anger and strength that we project on God, on the other. Take that strength, even if it looks negative: it is your strength. Be aware of it, own it, act God, and you'll break through your paralysing fear: you will be able to communicate with God, be able to listen to him and discover him.'
(*We Heard the Bird Sing*, 17-18)

In his spiritual therapy, de Mello does not attempt to emphasise a particular theology. It is not just a negative theology that he proposes, much less does he abandon the idea of a personal God. His whole aim is to liberate people from oppressive ideas of God and to emphasise a God of communication. 'You will be able to communicate with God, be able to listen to him and discover him.'

An attitude in Christian piety is to make use of God as one's crutch in life. Such a dependence on God is sometimes approved of as a form of saintliness. Father de Mello, however, does not share that opinion, as the following testimony demonstrates:

One day in 1986, Tony and I were walking along the causeway of Lonavla lake. It was my last meeting with him. The conversation turned to the topic of God: I spoke of my personal experience of God as Father, a loving Father, who meant so much in my life. Tony listened. At a certain moment he said: 'When are you going to let go of God, your God? You are using him as crutch, and you won't grow. Your life and your world will be of the crutches. Throw him out and see what happens.'

Throw him out? Fall back on my inner resources? Fall back on the God who is in me ? Do away with the religious practices which I do out of habit? Stop turning to the Bible and the catechism books for norms of conduct? Listen to the Spirit speaking within me? Test the memorised doctrines on the anvil of reason and experience? Trust myself into the hands of the Mystery which works mightily in the universe? 'One day you may say,' Tony said, 'I found God, I know him, he is so and so, he is there and there, he is in me, in creation, in the Eucharist ... That is a day of disaster for you because you will have found *your* God, *your* own projection, so pitiful and small. These gods – these idols – in turn keep us pitiful and small. We would fight for them. It is frightening to hear people talk and threaten with things they only 'believe'. They can be terrible ... Mystery dues not require defenders. Idols do. Mystery makes us humble.'

I have experienced the anxiety and the dangers and the rewards of throwing away crutches.

(*We Heard the Bird Sing*, 77-78)

Throw away the crutches and start to walk. Pull down the golden calf into fire and experience the living God. However, that task is not an easy one. Many would rather continue with crutches because it is safer and more comfortable than to walk with uncertainty on one's own feet. The idea of God in the form of an idol made of him is safer than a faceless God of freedom.

Freedom is the mark of a spiritual person; the freedom which allows one to walk upright knowing that God alone is one's support; the rock and refuge:

During one session of my maxi sadhana, Tony and I had the following dialogue.

A: I feel threatened by the prospect of being free and of leaving others free. And I resent you for imposing your views, brainwashing and throwing us into doubt.

T: The more free and secure I became, the less proselytising I did. Nobody can make you doubt or impose something on you. Indicate one area in which you want to be free.

A: God. I want to be free of this God-Father.

T: Tell me what that means.

A: I believe God loves me and cares for me. At the same time there is an uneasiness in me about him. I resent him.

T: Suppose God-Father is a myth, a concept to explain a reality that is ineffable. Now go beyond the myth and go to the Ineffable. In fantasy go as it were on a special journey, into the reality beyond the myth. What happens?

A: ... I feel myself go ... the others are far ... I feel strong and cold and a sense of missing ....

T: Stay with the sense of coldness, of missing, and that sense of strength.

THE NOTIFICATION

A: ... I am a robot with a warm flame inside which wants to spread.
T: Be the robot with the flame and stand in front of your dad. What happens? (We had earlier worked on my unfinished relationship with my dad.)
A: ... As I stand here I am irritated ... angry with my dad ... resentful ... I want to push him out of the way with my iron arm ... and then the flame in me dies ...
T: You were not in touch with the strength in you when you were in front of your dad. Be again in front of him and be in touch with the flame in you, with your strength.
A: ... The flame wants to grow ... I am frightened ... there is struggle in me ... will he extinguish it? ... I go blank ...
T: Do this again. Stand atone before your dad and recapture the flame. Spend time on this.
Slowly I discovered how my resentment of God-Father, of my dad, of Tony were all of a piece: it found its nourishment in a whole set of experiences and inherited images of God, and of self, of beliefs and principles regarding moral and social relationships. Becoming aware of these and freeing myself of them in small painful steps, I trust I am on my way to the Ineffable of which Tony spoke.
(*We Heard the Bird Sing*, 40-41)

It is disheartening that the *Notification* does not see this balanced and healthy teaching of Father de Mello. On the contrary, the *Explanatory Note* adds the following remark: '... criticism and frequent irony are directed towards any attempt at language of God.' At this point, the Vatican authors are a little amiss regarding Father Anthony de Mello's humour and satire. The *Notification* does not appreciate images or explanations of the concept of God taken from other religions and cultures and casts doubt on them, making an effort to show the fallacy of them when it sees them.

12. Scripture as a Road-Sign

NOTIFICATION

- (The radical apophatism) leads even to a denial that the Bible contains valid statements about God.

- The words of Scripture are indications which serve only to lead a person to silence.

- In other passages, the judgement on sacred religious texts, not excluding the Bible, becomes even more severe: they are said to prevent people from following their own common sense and cause them to become obtuse and cruel.

EXPLANATORY NOTE

- Nor do sacred scriptures, the Bible included, enable us to know God; they are simply like road-signs which tell me nothing about the city to which I am going: '... I come to a sign that says 'Bombay.' ... That sign isn't Bombay! Actually it doesn't even look like Bombay. It's not a picture of Bombay. It's a sign.'

- 'That is what the scriptures are, a sign.' (*Walking on Water*, 13) Continuing this metaphor, one could say that a road-sign becomes useless when I have reached my destination; this is what Father de Mello seems to be saying: 'The scripture is the excellent portion, the finger pointed toward the Light. We use its words to go beyond conceptions and reach silence.' (*Walking on Water*, 16)

- Paradoxically God's revelation is not expressed in his words, but in silence. (cf also *One Minute Wisdom*, 118, 157, 191, etc. *Awareness*, 101)

- 'In the Bible only the path is indicated to us, as in the Muslim, Buddhist scriptures, etc.' (*La iluminación es la espiritualidad*, 64)

THE NOTIFICATION

Father de Mello has not explicitly treated in his writings themes like 'Scriptures', either in reference to the Christian theology or with regard to spirituality. Whenever he mentioned Scripture, it was for a therapeutic or pedagogical purpose. He was speaking to Catholic religious men and women who knew the Scriptures but who needed a healthy attitude towards them in their daily life.

As I have pointed out above, what Father de Mello tries to underline in the case of Scriptures is not the contrast between a 'road-sign' and the 'city' (as apparently the *Notification* understands it) but the ignorance of those who identify the metallic or wooden plate of the road-sign with the city. For many people, the name of a city does not signify more than the word, which is its name. The city of Bombay is not the word 'Bombay'. Similarly, God is totally other than the word 'God'; Scriptures in their words and phrases are not the same as the Divine Message which these words and phrases communicate. Thereby Father de Mello does not teach something other than what the Catholic Church teaches and understands by Scriptures. They are the Word of God. But the Word is not the printed, written or spoken words. Father de Mello's thought is contrary to what the *Notification* and *La iluminacion* want Father de Mello to say, that in the Bible, 'only the path is indicated to us, as in Muslim and Buddhist scriptures'. There is a double misunderstanding here. The Roman text and *La iluminacion* apparently understand neither De Mello nor the Muslim and Buddhist scriptures. For, these do not teach that their Scriptures are mere indications of the path. They are for them both the path and the goal. Father De Mello and the Catholic Church wouldn't identify God's word with an 'Eternal Book that is in the presence of God', or where the book is God's spoken Word in its intonation and form. The Scriptures for the Catholic Church are God's Word in human words. And God speaks in all languages, not just in Hebrew, Greek or English. He speaks directly to the human heart.

It does not require much effort to see that Father de Mello's intention is not to belittle the Scriptures or to despise them as useless words, but to stress that one ought to go beyond the words used by the Scriptures and not remain struck to them verbatim. De Mello criticises those who pride themselves in the written word as the absolute and fixed expression of the ultimate reality. He wants to show that mere words of Scriptures are insufficient. There is a constant interrelation between the person and the Word of the scriptures: it is through faith that one captures the reality of the Word.

A story of Father de Mello that should have raised more problems had the *Notification* had knowledge of it:
A learned man once came to Buddha and said, 'The things you teach, sir, are not to be found in the Holy Scriptures.'
'Then put them in the Scriptures,' said Buddha.
After an embarrassed pause the man went on to say, 'May I be so bold as to suggest, sir, that some of the things you teach actually contradict the Holy Scriptures?'
'Then amend the Scriptures,' said Buddha.

A proposal was made at the United Nations that all Scriptures of all religions of the world be revised. Anything in them that would lead to intolerance or cruelty or bigotry should be deleted. Anything that would in any way be against the dignity and welfare of man should be dropped.
When it was found that the author was Jesus Christ himself, reporters rushed to his residence to ask him further explanation. His explanation was simple and brief: 'The Scriptures, like the Sabbath, are for man,' he said, 'Not man for the Scriptures.'
(*The Song of the Bird*, 61)

The allegory clearly points out that the emphasis is not at all on the Scriptures but on what people make out of them. The categorical accusation made by the *Notification* saying 'they [that is, religious texts not excluding the Bible] are said to prevent people from following their own common sense and cause them to become obtuse and cruel' is not justified by any passage from the writings of Father de Mello. I have ploughed through his writings to find if he ever said such things elsewhere, and I found no such saying or any allusion to it. I have the impression that the *Notification* wrongly attributes the words to Father de Mello, which are probably from some other author.

The mystic experience – the direct experience of God of which Father de Mello speaks – is a contentious issue. The mystic pays more importance to the experience God where God is to be found, rather than to confine himself and God to the framework of the Scriptures. Like the believers in Jesus said to the Samaritan woman: 'We believe now, not because of what you said, but because we ourselves have heard him, and we know that he really is the Saviour of the world' (John 4:42), the Christian confesses:

> I have been content to learn about you at second hand, Lord. From Scriptures and Saints; from Popes and preachers. I wish I could say to all of them, 'It is no longer because of what you said that I believe, for I have heard him myself.'
> (*The Song of the Bird*, 217)

Again, this criticism is not one of the Holy Father or of his cardinals. It is a forceful way of saying that the Scriptures become valid only when one really experiences God.

Regarding the second objection raised as to the road-sign becoming useless when one has reached the destination, I do not see why it should create a problem for the Catholic faith. Do we believe that we carry our Bibles along with us when we meet God? Aren't they crutches that one will throw away when one can walk?

I think what the *Notification* really finds difficult to accept is Father de Mello's presupposition that the Scriptures lead us to silence. That is the third objection raised in the passage above. We have already mentioned it when the *Notification* had raised the point earlier (cf p 97). This is certainly Father de Mello's teaching, but it does not contradict in any way the church's teaching. In fact, it can be a refreshing complement to it. But the references given by the *Explanatory Note*, except '*Awareness* 101,' are all incorrect. So one does not really know to which passages it refers. I guess it alludes to the text of the opening meditation in *Sadhana – A Way to God* (3-9) which we read and commented on earlier (ibid).

It should be observed that the objections raised are based on a misunderstanding of Father de Mello's teaching. Secondly, the texts cited in support are, for the most part, taken from the two problematic works wrongly ascribed to Father de Mello, of which I have already given my opinion.

The objections raised by the *Explanatory Note* analysed above are all a pernickety search to find arguments to condemn. The *Notification* overlooks the real teaching of Father de Mello and the real good he did for thousands of people who came to him for help. His teachings cannot be separated from the pastoral assistance that he brought, and this assistance never deviated or estranged people from the church or from the Christian faith. The *Notification* makes a grave error in attributing to Father de Mello texts that are not written by him. It fails to appreciate the real Catholic sense of Father de Mello's teaching.

13. Religions

NOTIFICATION

• Religions, including Christianity, are one of the major obstacles to the discovery of the truth.

EXPLANATORY NOTE

• Thus, what is proclaimed is an impersonal God who stands above all the religions, while objections are raised to the Christian proclamation of the God of love, held to be incompatible with the notion of the necessity of the Church for salvation: My friend and I went to the fair. *The World Fair of Religions ...* At the Jewish Stall we were given hand-outs that said that God was All-Compassionate and the Jews were his Chosen People. The Jews. No other people were as Chosen as the Jewish People. At the Moslem Stall we learnt that God was All-Merciful and Mohammed is his only Prophet. Salvation comes from listening to God's only Prophet. At the Christian Stall we discovered that God is Love and there is no salvation outside the Church. Join the Church or risk eternal damnation. On the way out I asked my friend, 'What do you think of God?' He replied, 'He is

> bigoted, fanatical and cruel.' Back home, I said to God, 'How do you put up with this sort of thing, Lord? Don't you see they have been giving you a bad name for centuries?' God said, 'I didn't organise the Fair. I'd be too ashamed to even visit it.' ('The World Fair of Religions' in *The Song of the Bird*, 186-187; cf ibid., 189-190, 195)
>
> • The teaching of the Church on God's universal salvific will and on the salvation of non-Christians is not presented correctly, nor is the Christian message of God as Love: 'God is love. And he loves and rewards us forever if we observe his commandments.' 'If?' said the Master, 'Then the news isn't all that good, is it?' (*One Minute Nonsense*, 198; cf ibid, 206).

The accusation made by the *Notification*, 'Religions, including Christianity, are one of the major obstacles to the discovery of truth,' cannot be attributed to Father de Mello. That idea is totally foreign to his thought, particularly when one surveys his works in their entirety. He never entertained thoughts against the church nor held a position that was not in accord with the mind of the church. He was always a faithful and good servant of her throughout his life, trained 'to think with the church' as Ignatius of Loyola would teach. The *Notification* does not bring any quotation from de Mello. It is therefore a false accusation.

The objections brought are that de Mello does not consider the necessity of the church for salvation and that he questions the 'God of Love'. His idea of the church and its necessity for salvation will be treated in a later chapter. We limit ourselves here to reflections on de Mello's attitude towards religion.

First of all, de Mello's story, as quoted in the *Explanatory Note*, needs to be read carefully. It is not against Christianity nor against any other religion. Furthermore, one cannot conclude that 'For him, to think that the God of one's own religion is the only one is simply fanaticism.' The point that De Mello makes is exclusively over the masquerade of religions in a 'fair of religions' that people make of religions today. Religions are often no more the 'good news to men' but fortresses of doctrine whereby men try to defend their own points of view and interests. God does not organise such a fair. He is ashamed to visit it. There is a difference between God organising a 'religion' and God organising the 'fair of religions.' The fair is the human parody.

It is not just Christianity that proclaims to teach the absolute truth. Other religions also claim to be the absolute paths to salvation. The Muslim is convinced that the true Revelation has come down only in the Koran and that salvation is available to humanity only through submission to God as taught by the Koran and the Prophet. There is no Law (Dharma) greater or better than the Law of the Wheel, teaches Buddha. The Hindu teachings, like in the Bhagavadgita, holds that all worship given to the different deities are addressed in reality to the supreme Lord (*Bhagavaan*), who alone is the salvation and liberation from bondage for the entire humankind.

The first question that one needs to raise at this point is what is the meaning of this claim for absolute truth asserted by all religions? Why does each religion claim to be the exclusive way of salvation? A close look at these teachings seems to point out that such exclusive teachings are not developed in order to put down or suppress similar claims of other religions or to use this teaching as a slogan against other believers. The purpose of the exclusive claims appear to be solely for the internal use of the faithful of a religion; to confirm and affirm them in the choice of their faith and to set before them a way of salvation that is sure and safe.

Today, in the context of inter-religious dialogue and intercultural meeting of nations, we are invited to exercise a responsible attitude towards humanity and towards all religions. No religion may preach a doctrine that will humiliate, belittle and reduce other faiths and faithful to an inferior level. The semitic religions have in the past often succumbed to this temptation. Such an attitude has provoked war and destruction. It will not serve for peace and harmony among present-day societies. The practice of faith entails a social responsibility.

While it is normal for a religion to develop the absolute claim for truth in its conviction of faith, it makes a parody of itself when it blindly affirms its superiority over others. Faith is not a measure to compare religions, its purpose is not to judge and condemn. Faith engenders charity and hope, the gift of God to enliven and foster life on earth.

The *Notification* confuses religion and the masquerade of religion. It misses Father de Mello's point of criticism of religions in which each religion brandishes its truth as the only truth for all people, thereby implying that other 'truths' are false.

14. TRUTH AND FANATICISM

NOTIFICATION

• This truth, however, is never defined by the author in its precise contents. For him, to think that the God of one's own religion is the only one is simply fanaticism. 'God' is considered as a cosmic reality, vague and omnipresent; the personal nature of God is ignored and in practice denied. (2)

EXPLANATORY NOTE

• Every concrete religion is an obstacle to arriving at the truth. Furthermore, what is said about the Scriptures is said also about religion in general: 'All fanatics wanted to catch hold of their God and make him the only one.' (*La iluminación es la espiritualidad*, 65; cf ibid, 28, 30) What matters is the truth, whether it comes from Buddha or from Mohammed, since 'the important thing is to discover the truth where all truths come together, because truth is one' (ibid, 65) 'Most people, alas, have enough religion to hate but not enough to love.' (*Prayer of the Frog I*, 104; cf ibid, 33, 94) When the obstacles that prevent one from seeing reality are listed, religion comes first: 'First your beliefs. If you experience life as a communist or a capitalist, as a Moslem or a Jew, you are experiencing life in a prejudiced, slanted way; there is a barrier, a layer of fat between Reality and you because you no longer see and touch it directly.' (*Call to Love*, 30-31) 'If all human beings were fitted with such hearts, people would no longer think of themselves as Communists or Capitalists, as Christians or Muslims or Buddhists. The very clarity of their thinking would show them that all thinking, all concepts, all beliefs are lamps full of darkness, signs of their ignorance.' (ibid, 94; cf also *One Minute Wisdom*, 159, 217, on the dangers of religion.) What is asserted about religion is also said concretely about the Scriptures. (cf *The Song of the Bird*, 186ff; *One Minute Nonsense*, 19)

The question of truth in Father de Mello's writings is raised here. Father de Mello does not, in fact, make frequent use of the term 'truth' in its philosophical sense. For his truth is the existential reality touching the life of all. He underlines deviations and misuse of it found in all life situations, including religions. So the accusation that he 'does not define this truth' appears to be somewhat strange. I do not think that Father de Mello would have ever ventured to define it simply for the fact that he did not indulge in philosophical and epistemological discussions. Truth meant, for him, like for his renowned countryman, Mahatma Gandhi, an existential, practical reality for the good of all; an experience to live, more than to indulge in definitions. For, ultimately, it is not the definition of truth that binds or liberates but truth lived in life. In this context Father de Mello reports a painful incident:

> In his autobiography, Mahatma Gandhi tells how in his student days in South Africa he became deeply interested in the Bible, especially the Sermon on the Mount.
> He become convinced that Christianity was the answer to the caste system that had plagued India for centuries, and he seriously considered becoming a Christian.
> One day he went to a church to attend Mass and get instructions. He was stopped at the entrance and gently told that if he desired to attend Mass he was welcome to do so in a church reserved for blacks.
> He left and never returned.
> (*The Prayer of the Frog I*, 105)

The truth was evident and needed no definition. Gandhi could not see the truth in a church that builds two churches to celebrate Mass, one for whites and another for blacks. It was worse than the caste system in his own religion. That is the kind of truth of which de Mello speaks in his writings: that which, in many instances, disturbs the conscience of those 'good Christians' who have learnt to define truth but not to practise it.

The second reproach of the *Notification* is, 'For him, to think that the God of one's own religion is the only one is simply fanaticism.' The fanaticism lies not in the belief in one God as the only and true God. As I have just pointed out above, each religion teaches its God as the only and true God, just as one would consider one's mother as the best woman on earth. The fanaticism comes up when the so-called believer draws out his fang of intolerance and, while professing his faith in one God, tries to suppress or de-class the God of the other. The fact is that 'my mother is the best woman on earth' is gladly admitted and accepted by all; it does not imply that other mothers or women are of a lesser value.

However, 'God is considered as a cosmic reality, vague and omnipresent' are not Father de Mello's words. He has never spoken of God as a 'vague' thing. If he sometimes developed an apophatic language, it was not meant to develop an impersonal idea of God, but just the opposite: to shake up those who were, in their belief, a bit too habituated towards a God who is reduced to human dimensions.

The *Explanatory Note* has recourse to *La Iluminacion* to adduce texts against de Mello. I will not comment on these for the reason I have already discussed. These are not thoughts of de Mello.

On the contrary, the references made to *The Prayer of the Frog*: 'Most people, alas, have enough religion to hate but not enough to love' (*Prayer of the Frog I* 104) is a typical de Mello thought, but it needs to be placed within its proper context. It is not a general and overall affirmation made but a moral deduced from a concrete story, which is as follows:

> A hunter sent his dog after something that moved behind the trees. It chased out a fox and corralled it into a position where the hunter could shoot it.
> The dying fox said to the hound, 'Were you never told that the fox is brother to the dog?'
> 'I was, indeed,' said the dog. 'But that's for idealists and fools. For the practical-minded, brotherhood is created by identity of interests.'
>
> Said the Christian to the Buddhist: 'We could be brothers, really. But that's for idealists and fools. For the practical minded, brotherhood lies in identity of beliefs.'
> Most people, alas, have enough religion to hate but not enough to love.
> (*The Prayer of the Frog I*, 104)

Unfortunately, religions seem to divide more than they unite. Not that a religion seeks to spread disharmony or hate; its religious ideology and tenets, preached with fanaticism, estrange its believers from believers of other religions. A Christian feels out of place in a Hindu sacrifice, uncomfortable in the company of monks meditating and barred from prayer in a mosque. Should I separate myself in my heart and mind from a person of another religion just because he adheres to another belief? De Mello says that in the way we practise our religions, we produce more hate than love.

The second text quoted is the story of the Forest Church, which is a beautiful allegorical narrative to explain why God hides things from our eyes. The story wants to say that God does not, in fact, hide things but puts them right before our eyes, so close that we fail to see them:

> Once upon a time there was a forest where the birds sang by day and the insects by night. Trees flourished, flowers bloomed and all manner of creatures roamed about in freedom.
> And all who entered there were led to Solitude which is the home of God who dwells in Nature's silence and Nature's beauty.
> But then the Age of Unconsciousness arrived when it became possible for people to construct buildings a thousand feet high and to destroy rivers and forests and mountains in a month. So houses of worship were built from the wood of the forest trees and from the stone under the forest soil. Pinnacle, spire and minaret pointed towards the sky; the air was filled with the sound of bells, with prayer and chant and exhortation.
> And God was suddenly without a home.
> God *hides* things by putting them *before* our eyes!
> (*The Prayer of the Frog I*, 33)

This beautiful myth does not speak about truth or fanaticism. It is on the blindness of human beings who, out of their selfish interest in possessing, fail to see God's presence in nature, destroy it and fill it with idols of their own making. Nature has an important place in Father de Mello's spirituality. Yet such a nature-centred view, as one might doubt, does not lead him to an impersonal or cosmic language. God is the living Person in and behind nature.

> A third text adduced, I must admit, is somewhat problematic:
> Said a preacher to a friend, 'We have just had the greatest revival our church has experienced in many years.'
> 'How many did you add to your church membership?'
> 'None. We lost five hundred.'
> Jesus would have applauded!
> Experience shows, alas, that our religious convictions bear as much relation to our personal holiness as a man's dinner jacket to his digestion.
> (*The Prayer of the Frog I*, 94)

The story comes from a time when de Mello was a young Jesuit filled with missionary zeal. It was a time when the missionary success in India and elsewhere was gauged by the number of conversions obtained every year. One did not care very much about the quality of the Christian life, which was not the central issue ('jacket to digestion'). The whole interest was to gain the greatest number of conversions. Losing membership can also be a sign of renewal and deepening of faith when people become conscious of the demands of their engagement with the faith or shocked by the lethargy of those who preach it. The story somewhat shocks our pragmatic missionary interests, but it does not say that converting people is an act of fanaticism.

The passage from *Call to Love* (30-31) quoted above contains an idea central to de Mello's teaching on how beliefs, ideas, habits, attachments and fears can act as thick buffers that hinder the access to the core of the matter. It is culled from a meditation on Matthew 24:1-2: 'When his disciples came to point out to him the building of the temple, he answered them 'You see all these, do you not? Truly, I say to you, there will not be left here one stone upon another that will not be thrown down'.' What Jesus and Tony de Mello say is that beliefs and the rest can be a hindrance if one sticks to the exterior form of the 'belief's formula' just as one sticks to the exterior form of religious buildings, which are symbols of human achievement. The life of faith is modelled on the life of Jesus by ever questioning one's certitudes and values in life, building (but also pulling down) and not being ashamed of the cross. It would be too simple to quote this passage as a critique against Christianity preaching a sort of fanaticism. Father de Mello gave this meditation to his Jesuit brethren and to religious people, some of whom were 'covered with layers of fat till it becomes too dull and lazy to think, to observe, to explore, to discover'. (p 30)

Continuing in the same line of thought, the *Explanatory Note* quotes page 94, but it omits the most important sentence which follows the text quoted: 'And in that realisation the walls of their separate wells would collapse and they would be invaded by the ocean that unites all people in the truth.' There is something very important here to be noted for the future of dogmatic expressions and so-called interreligious dialogue. Our dogmas and also our religious identity have the sole purpose of fostering peace, love and life among men and women of the world, and not separating them. They have to be lived in such a way that

THE NOTIFICATION

they help to grow more and more in the truth and love of life and not in mutual condemnation and war. This awareness is that which de Mello advocated.

There is an error in the following two references given in the *Explanatory Note*: In *One Minute Wisdom*, page 159 carries only the sketch of a tree and page 217 gives the nice little story that follows:

> Said the disappointed visitor. 'Why has my stay here yielded no fruit?'
> 'Could it be because you lacked the courage to shake the tree?' said the master benignly.

Is it the wrong reference to the source or is the *Notification* against 'shaking the tree'?

Further, the *Explanatory Note* sums up: 'What is asserted about religion is also said concretely about the Scriptures.' *The Song of the Bird* pp 186ff are not stories against Scriptures; they are about religious fanaticism. *One Minute Nonsense*, page 19, is, in fact, a nonsensical de Mello story to laugh at and not to be taken as an offence against the Scriptures:

> 'When you speak about Reality,' said the Master, 'you are attempting to put the Inexpressible into words, so your words are certain to be misunderstood.' Thus people who read that expression of Reality called the Scriptures become stupid and cruel for they follow, not their common sense, but what they think their Scriptures say. He had the perfect parable to show this:
> A village blacksmith found an apprentice willing to work hard at low pay. The smith immediately began his instructions to the lad: 'When I take the metal out of the fire, I'll lay it on the anvil; and when I nod my head you hit it with the hammer.' The apprentice did precisely what he thought he was told.
> Next day he was the village blacksmith.

I come now to a major point raised by the *Notification*: the Jesus Christ of Anthony de Mello. I must confess from the very outset my pain felt at my Roman Catholic Church authorities who denigrate a man who was not only a faithful disciple of Jesus but who brought a large number of people to come to love Jesus as their Saviour and Lord, the Son of God who reveals the Father. At no time in his life did de Mello show doubt toward this unswerving faith in Jesus Christ. Neither the Society of Jesus, the church in India nor his numerous hearers ever got the idea that he was preaching a Jesus Christ that was different from the teachings of the Catholic Church. The texts that the *Notification* adduces are all fished out mainly from the writings wrongly attributed to de Mello. It places them out of context and falsely interprets them. It is outrageous that the teachers of the Catholic Church so estrange a saint who was a disciple and intimate friend of Jesus Christ.

15. JESUS CHRIST

NOTIFICATION

- Father de Mello demonstrates an appreciation for Jesus, of whom he declares himself to be a 'disciple'. But he considers Jesus as a master alongside others. The only difference from other men is that Jesus is 'awake' and fully free, while others are not.

- Jesus is not recognised as the Son of God, but simply as the one who teaches that all people are children of God.

EXPLANATORY NOTE

- The divine sonship of Jesus is diluted into the notion of the divine sonship of all men: 'To which God replied, 'A feast day is holy because it shows that all the days of the year are holy. And a sanctuary is holy because it shows that all places are sanctified. So Christ was born to show that all men are sons of God.' (*The Song of the Bird*, 189). Father de Mello certainly manifests a personal adherence to Christ, of whom he declares himself a disciple (*Wellsprings,122*), in whom he has faith (ibid,113) and whom he personally encounters. (ibid,115ff, 124ff). His presence is transfiguring (cf ibid, 92ff). But other statements are disconcerting. Jesus is mentioned as one teacher among many: 'Lao Tzu and Socrates, Buddha and Jesus, Zarathustra and Mohammed. (*One Minute Wisdom*, 2). Jesus on

THE NOTIFICATION

the cross appears as the one who has freed himself perfectly of everything:

- 'I see the Crucified as stripped of everything: Stripped of his dignity ... Stripped of his reputation ... Stripped of support ... Stripped of his God ... As I gaze at that lifeless body I slowly understand that I am looking at the symbol of supreme and total liberation. In being fastened to the cross Jesus becomes alive and free ... So now I contemplate the majesty of the man who has freed himself from all that makes us slaves, destroys our happiness ...' (*Wellsprings*, 95-97).

- Jesus on the cross is the man free of all ties; thus he becomes the symbol of interior liberation from everything to which we were attached. But isn't Jesus something more than a man who is free? Is Jesus my saviour or does he simply direct me toward a mysterious reality which has saved him? 'Will I ever get in touch, Lord, with the source from which your words and wisdom flow? ... Will I ever find the wellsprings of your courage?' (*Wellsprings*, 123). 'The lovely thing about Jesus was that he was so at home with sinners, because he understood that he wasn't one bit better than they were' ... The only difference between Jesus and those others was that he was awake and they weren't.' (*Awareness*, 30-31; cf also *La iluminación es la espiritualidad*, 30, 62). Christ's presence in the Eucharist is but a symbol that refers to a deeper reality: his presence in creation. 'The whole of creation is the body of Christ, and you believe that it is only in the Eucharist. The Eucharist indicates this creation. The Body of Christ is everywhere and yet you only notice its symbol which indicates to you what is essential, namely life.' (*La iluminación es la espiritualidad*, 61).

In order to better follow the *Notification*'s critique regarding this point, I have re-arranged the text under sub-headings, each point corresponding to its explanatory note, whenever that was possible. The sub-headings are mine.

NOTIFICATION	EXPLANATORY NOTE
1. *Father de Mello's appreciation of Jesus*	
• Father de Mello demonstrates an appreciation for Jesus, of whom he declares himself to be a 'disciple'.	• Father de Mello certainly manifests a personal adherence to Christ, of whom he declares himself a disciple (*Wellsprings*, 122), in whom he has faith (ibid,113) and who he personally encounters (ibid,115ff, 124ff). His presence is transfiguring (cf ibid, 92ff).

THE NOTIFICATION

2. Jesus as master alongside others

• But he considers Jesus a master alongside others.

• But other statements are disconcerting. Jesus is mentioned as one teacher among many: 'Lao Tzu and Socrates, Buddha and Jesus, Zarathustra and Mohammed. (*One Minute Wisdom*, 2)

3. The only difference between Jesus and others

• The only difference from other men is that Jesus is 'awake' and fully free, while others are not.

• Jesus on the cross appears as the one who has freed himself perfectly of everything:

• I see the Crucified as stripped of everything: Stripped of his dignity ... Stripped of his reputation ... Stripped of support ... Stripped of his God ... As I gaze at that lifeless body I slowly understand that I am looking at the symbol of supreme and total liberation. In being fastened to the cross Jesus becomes alive and free ... So now I contemplate the majesty of the man who has freed himself from all that makes us slaves, destroys our happiness ... (*Wellsprings*, 95-97).

• Jesus on the cross is the man free of all ties; thus he becomes the symbol of interior liberation from everything to which we were attached. But isn't Jesus something more than a man who is free? Is Jesus my saviour or does he simply direct me toward a mysterious reality which has saved him? 'Will

I ever get in touch, Lord, with the source from which your words and wisdom flow? ... Will I ever find the wellsprings of your courage?' (*Wellsprings*, 123). 'The lovely thing about Jesus was that he was so at home with sinners, because he understood that he wasn't one bit better than they were' ...

• 'The only difference between Jesus and those others was that he was awake and they weren't.' (*Awareness*, 30-31); cf also *La iluminación es la espiritualidad*, 30, 62).

4. Jesus is not recognised as the Son of God

• Jesus is not recognised as the Son of God, but simply as the one who teaches that all people are children of God.

• The divine sonship of Jesus is diluted into the notion of the divine sonship of all men: 'To which God replied, 'A feast day is holy because it shows that all the days of the year are holy. And a sanctuary is holy because it shows that all places are sanctified. So Christ was born to show that all men are sons of God.' (*The Song of the Bird*, 189).

5. Christ's presence in the Eucharist is but a symbol

• Christ's presence in the Eucharist is but a symbol that refers to a deeper reality: his presence in creation. "The whole of creation is the body of Christ, and you believe that it is only in the Eucharist. The Eucharist indicates this creation. The Body of Christ is everywhere and yet you only

> notice its symbol which indicates to you what is essential, namely life.' (*La iluminación es la espiritualidad*, 61).

The *Notification* and *Explanatory Note* clearly recognise Father de Mello's allegiance and personal adherence to Jesus Christ as his master. But then it points out more theological issues in which his teaching is declared to be wanting, particularly the question of recognising Jesus as the Son of God. For those of us who knew Tony personally, heard his teachings and lived with him, there was not even the least suspicion that he could have entertained a concept of Christ different from that of the church. One needs only to flip through the pages of Father de Mello's works to see the central spotlight he gives to Jesus Christ in his meditations and writings, his Christ-centred spirituality. The presence of Jesus Christ is so preponderant in his works that, in this methodological approach, any passage that might appear to draw a picture of Christ other than that which is put forth by the church should be interpreted in the light of his general and fundamental teaching on Jesus Christ rather than being hastily concluded to be 'heretical'. Furthermore, the pedagogical and therapeutic contexts of his teachings are of the utmost importance in any interpretation.

Father de Mello's concept of Jesus Christ is imbued by Jesuit spirituality and its approach to the person of Jesus. In his *Spiritual Exercises* as well as in all his other teachings, Ignatius of Loyola did not teach his companions a 'theology' of Jesus Christ in christological terms of the Councils of the church. He taught his followers to be like Jesus, *Jesu-ita*, which meant the imitation of Jesus in 'body and soul'. In the *Spiritual Exercises* the Jesuit is asked to imitate Jesus who walked on the streets of Palestine and went about doing good, who suffered and died on the cross and rose again, he who was God, Saviour and Redeemer of humanity, always seeking a personal intimacy with Jesus as friend, elder brother, master, Lord and Saviour. This is what Father de Mello taught. This image of Jesus was amply clear to his religious audience who did not demand a theological exactitude in a lived spirituality.

Let me give an example. In *Sadhana – A Way to God*, one repeatedly finds phrases like the following:

Now place yourself and this object in the presence of Jesus Christ, the Word of God, in whom and for whom everything was made. Listen to what he has to say to you and to the object ... What do the two of you say in response?
(*Sadhana – A Way to God*, 51)

The personal relationship with God and with Jesus Christ is perhaps most powerfully emphasised in one of his meditations entitled 'The Empty Chair'. One can observe there the simplicity of the prayer that Father de Mello teaches, the 'application of the senses' that is taught in the *Spiritual Exercises*. Father de Mello first recounts the story of a priest who went to visit a sick person in his home:

He noticed an empty chair at the patient's bedside and asked what it was doing there. The patient said, 'I had placed Jesus on that chair and was talking to him before you arrived ... For years I found it extremely difficult to pray until a friend explained to me that prayer was a matter of talking to Jesus. He told me to place an empty chair nearby, to imagine Jesus sitting on that chair and to speak with him and listen to what he says to me in reply. I've had no difficulty praying ever since.'

Some days later, so the story goes, the daughter of the patient came to the rectory to inform the priest that her father had died. She said, 'I left him alone for a couple of hours. He seemed so peaceful. When I got back to the room I found him dead. I noticed a strange thing, though: his head was resting not on the bed but on a chair that was beside his bed.'

Then Father de Mello continues:

Try this exercise yourself right now, even though at first it might seem childish to you:
Imagine you see Jesus sitting close to you. In doing this you are putting your imagination at the service of your faith: Jesus isn't here in the way you are imagining him, but he certainly is here and your imagination helps to make you aware of this.
Now speak to Jesus ... If no one is around, speak out in a soft

voice ...
Listen to what Jesus says to you in reply ... or what you imagine him to say ...
If you do not know what exactly to say to Jesus, narrate to him all the events of the past day and give him your comment on each of them. That is the difference between thinking and praying.
(*Sadhana – A Way to God*, 72)

The Empty Chair is only one example in a series of clearly-written meditations meant to bring people to the Person of our Lord Jesus Christ. Elsewhere, he tries to revive the Catholic teachings on the Sacred Heart of Jesus, a task especially entrusted to the Society of Jesus, and the commitment to Jesus in love:

The devotion to the Heart of Christ, so vigorous some years ago, so much on the decline today, would flourish once again if people would understand that it consists essentially in accepting Jesus Christ as love incarnate, as the manifestation of the unconditional love of God for us.
(*Sadhana – A Way to God*, 116)

De Mello attributes 'fruits beyond all his expectations' in his own prayer life and apostolate issuing from this unconditional love of God which is the meaning of the Sacred Heart:

It is customary at retreats for retreatants to ask themselves those three questions made famous by the *Spiritual Exercises* of St Ignatius: 'What have I done for Christ? What am I doing for Christ? What am I going to do for Jesus Christ?' The answer to the third question generally takes the form of all sorts of generous actions and sacrifices that the retreatant desires to perform as an expression of his love for Christ. My suggestion to retreatants is this: there is nothing you can do for Christ that will give him greater pleasure than that you believe in his love, his unconditional love for you.
(*Sadhana – A Way to God*, 116)

In his therapies, Jesus Christ was also often the central question:
I was not getting out of life what I knew it was offering me. On the contrary I felt life increasingly to be a burden, a drag. I was handling some of my problems poorly.

ANTHONY DE MELLO

When I told Tony about this it was actually my first meeting with him – he asked me to imagine I was sitting with Christ and Christ was asking me to describe my finest qualities. I did. I thought I was quite generous in praise of my talents. Then Tony asked me to tell Jesus my faults, etc ...

At the end of the exercise Tony said that I was much more eloquent in reciting my faults than I was in outlining my good qualities.

Simple as this interaction was, it somehow brought about in me a major shift. That was the beginning for me of waking up, of awareness.

(*We Heard the Bird Sing*, 23)

His last work, *Call to Love*, is a masterpiece of Christ-centred spirituality. Each chapter of this work is a new christological interpretation based on a gospel saying of Jesus. He pictures Jesus Christ as the 'God-living-among-us,' whom the traditional christology had too-often couched in learned but lifeless formulas. He brings Jesus Christ to modern life and its spiritual problems, awakening in the reader the 'force of life' that Jesus is. Given these spiritual teachings on Jesus Christ in his earlier writings as well as in his later ones, it is simply unimaginable that Father de Mello could have taught something that could be dangerous to the Christian faith.

However, let one now turn to the other objections raised by the Roman *Notification*.

Jesus as master alongside others
The *Notification* and the *Explanatory Note* raise the grave accusation that Father de Mello reduces Jesus to the status of a master, just one among other masters. In support of its claim, the *Explanatory Note* makes reference to *One Minute Wisdom*, page two. However, the reference is not exact. Most likely, it refers to page VIII, as follows:

The Master in these tales is not a single person. He is a Hindu Guru, A Zen Roshi, a Taoist Sage, a Jewish Rabbi, a Christian Monk, a Sufi Mystic. He is Lao Tzu and Socrates, Buddha and Jesus, Zarathustra and Mohammed. His teaching is found in the 7th century BC and the 20th century AD. His

wisdom belongs to East and West alike. Do his historical antecedents really matter? History, after all, is the record of appearances, not Reality; of doctrines, not of Silence.
(*One Minute Wisdom*, VIII)

Enumerating Jesus among other masters does not signify, as we have noted in the previous chapter, that one reduces him to their status in his being and in his teachings. It all depends on the context. For example, when the Holy Father prays at Assisi or elsewhere in the company of other religious leaders, it does not mean that the Christianity he represents is levelled to other religions. In today's multi-religious and inter-religious context, there is no other way than to place ourselves among others. Any other attitude can be misleading and give rise to unnecessary feelings of a superiority that is completely uncalled for. Let us not forget that Father de Mello wrote these words in India, where immense populations of different religions, in which Christianity is only a very small minority, live and work together. In such a context, to separate Jesus from other masters would give the impression of haughtiness and arrogance on the part of the Christians; an attitude that would make Jesus' image quite distasteful. There is no other way to go about proclaiming Jesus than to imitate the one shown by Jesus himself, who, as his apostle Paul attests, 'though he was in the form of God, did not count equality with God a thing to be grasped, but emptied himself, taking the form of a servant, being born in the likeness of men. And being found in human form he humbled himself and became obedient unto death, even death on a cross (Philippians 2:5-9). Following this example of Jesus, Christians and the church as a whole would gain more respect and love among the different people and religions of the world by humbly and truly placing themselves as one among others than by taking a haughty and defensive attitude of absolute superiority over others. One will show one's true superiority by excelling in one's humility.

The only difference between Jesus and others
Father de Mello's mystical contemplation of Jesus hanging on the cross, the symbol of supreme and total liberation of man free

from all ties and attachments, creates a deep apprehension in the minds of the authors of the *Notification*: 'Isn't Jesus something more than a man who is free? Is Jesus my Saviour or does he simply direct me toward a mysterious reality which has saved him?' The passage to which this debate refers is *Wellsprings*, (pp 95-97), a beautifully-written meditation on the Kenosis, that is, the 'emptying', of which Saint Paul speaks in the verse quoted above. It is Jesus, the man that is brought down to this emptiness at the event of Good Friday when death apparently subdued man. But this emptying does not deprive him of the Resurrection, which glorifies his divinity. Father de Mello experienced, as do all who are engaged in active pastoral work, that people are readier to accept Jesus as God than man. They would rather see him in his glory than one become like man, taking up our humanity. The fact that Father de Mello occasionally makes use of the term 'man' for Jesus does not mean that he forgets Jesus as God. The *Explanatory Note* emphasises the word 'man', whereas Father de Mello stresses the idea of 'freedom' even in the torments of suffering.

If Anthony de Mello did not theologically expatiate on the theme of the Saviour and Redeemer, it was not because he did not believe in it. Rather, it was simply unnecessary for him to do so for his audience, who were mostly composed of religious. These people were very aware of this aspect of their faith and needed no theological discourse about it. Conversely, they needed to see and feel the humanity of Jesus and to experience what it meant to be detached from one's attachments.

However, Anthony de Mello does amply speak of Jesus as Saviour. A clear statement can be found in his book, *Sadhana – A Way to God*, 124, where he proposes the meditation, Exercise 42: Jesus the Saviour. The opening words are:

> This is another form of practising the Jesus Prayer. The recitation of the name of Jesus not only brings the presence of Jesus with it but also brings the salvation of Jesus to the one who is praying. Jesus is essentially the Saviour. That is what his name means. (Mt 1:21) 'Salvation is to be found through him alone; for there is no one else in all the world whose name God has given to men by whom we can be saved.' (Acts 4:12)

THE NOTIFICATION

> The loving recitation of the name of Jesus makes Jesus present to us. When Jesus becomes present he gives us his salvation. What kind of salvation? The salvation he brought in Palestine two thousand years ago: Healing for all our illnesses, physical, emotional and spiritual; and, as a result, peace with our fellow men and with God and with ourselves.

Anthony de Mello wrote these words not at the beginning of his priestly ministry but, rather, later when his contact with other religions and cultures had brought about a spiritual growth in him. Furthermore, he had previously written the following in his book, *Contact with God*:

> The kind of madness that seizes the church when, on the vigil of Easter, she speaks of the sin of Adam as a 'necessary sin', as a 'happy fault', because it brought us our saviour Jesus Christ. She is only echoing what St Paul says to the Romans. Where sin abounded, grace superabounded.
> (*Contact with God*, 130-31)

Three other meditations in the same work should dispel all doubt regarding Father de Mello's faith in Jesus Christ as Saviour. In chapter fourteen, he discusses the kingdom of Christ and the intense attachment that a worker of the kingdom should have for the Person of Jesus Christ. Furthermore, chapter fifteen is entitled, 'To Know, to Love, to Follow Christ'. Finally, under, 'To know Christ', he writes that to call Jesus 'my Saviour' is a deep act of faith and not a mere verbal statement:

> 'It is no longer because of what you said that we believe, for we have heard him ourselves; and we know that this is in truth the Saviour of the World.' This is the aspiration of every priest, catechist, teacher of the gospels: that our audience should say to us, 'It is no longer because of what you have said that we believe, for we have seen and heard him ourselves.' This is the kind of knowledge of Christ that I am speaking of. A knowledge that is imparted by Christ himself, not by books or preachers.
> (*Contact with God*, 159-60)

This intimate and personal contact with Jesus as my Saviour is the object of the following meditative exercise:

> In my prayer today I face a vital question:
> Who is Jesus Christ for me?
> I begin by imagining myself to be in his presence
> – a presence that allows me to be totally myself.
> I then conduct a dialogue with him,
> taking for subject matter
> the titles scripture gives him:
> The first one is connected with his name: Saviour.
> Has Jesus been a saviour to me?
> In what circumstances?
> On what occasions?
> When I address him by this title,
> what meaning does it have? ...
> I share with him my answers to these questions ... he responds.
> (*Wellsprings*, 115)

Chapter sixteen is the concluding 'Meditation on the Life of Christ', where Anthony de Mello brings out the typical Jesuit spiritual approach to Jesus, that's to say, to become *alter Christus*, meaning 'second Christ'.

This deep faith in Jesus Christ is central to Anthony de Mello's spirituality. In addition it must be said that nowhere in his life or in his writings, even in his later and last writings or teachings, did he ever retract from it in words or deeds and never did he doubt that Jesus is our God and Saviour.

The *Notification* raises another major objection: '... the only difference from other men is that Jesus is awake and fully free while the others are not' (*Awareness* 30-31). When, however, this sentence is read in the context in which Father de Mello puts it, it seems to fit in well with the Christian teaching:

> To me selfishness seems to come out of an instinct for self-preservation, which is our deepest and first instinct. How can we opt for selflessness? It would be almost like opting for non being. Whatever it is, I am saying: Stop feeling bad about being selfish; we're all the same. Someone once had a terribly beautiful thing to say about Jesus. This person wasn't even Christian. He said: 'The lovely thing about Jesus was that he was so at home with sinners, because he understood that he

wasn't one bit better than they were.' We differ from others – from criminals, for example – only in what we do or don't do, not in what we are. The only difference between Jesus and the others was that he was awake and they weren't.
(*Awareness*, 30-31)

It's quite probable that the Vatican authors are reminded in this context of the Italian priest Don Mario Mazzoleni who was excommunicated a few years ago. Mazzoleni became a faithful disciple of Sai Baba, a renowned Guru in India, began to preach in his parish that his master, Sai Baba, was an incarnation of God just like Jesus Christ. The frequent affirmation of Sai Baba, '... the only difference between me and you is that I am awake, you are not' sounds similar to Father de Mello's words quoted above, but taken out of context.

However, what does de Mello mean in the above passage by Jesus 'being awake'? The Awakening of Jesus is one thing and the awakening of human beings is another. Jesus was aware of his divinity at all times and, therefore, could not have sinned. That was the big difference between Jesus and mankind: divine awareness. Man, too, will come to that state of awareness and awakening; to the state of sinlessness; that day man will be awake before God. The Catholic Church sees in Mary, Mother of God, the 'first fruits' of this final state. Mary was Immaculate, that is, free from sin. So, assumed into heaven, God accomplished in her what he has promised for mankind. We grow in hope towards the acquisition of this gift.

The Roman text alludes to *Iluminaciôn*, pages thirty and sixty-two but does not quote the texts. It is once again probable that it refers to one of its author's fantasies.

Jesus is not recognised as the Son of God
The *Notification* comes to this conclusion apparently because of a remark de Mello makes at the end of a story in '*The Song of the Bird*', p 188:

I went right back to the Religion Fair. This time I heard a speech of the High Priest of the Balakri Religion. The Prophet Balakri, we were told, was the Messiah born in the fifth century Holy Land of Mesambia.

I had another encounter with God that night. 'You're a great Discriminator aren't you God?' Why does the fifth century have to be the enlightened century and why does Mesambia have to be the holy land? Why do you discriminate against other centuries and other lands? What's wrong with my century for instance? And what's wrong with my land?'
To which God replied, 'A feast day is holy
because it shows that all the days
of the year are holy. And a sanctuary is
holy because it shows that all places are sanctified. So Christ was born to show that all men are sons of God.

Father de Mello does not try to equate the sonship of Jesus Christ with the sonship to which men and women are called. He does not enter into the theological distinction between Jesus as Son of God and the humans as the adoptive sons through faith. What he tries to point out in the above story is the universality of God's action among men. He does not discriminate among people. In his eyes, all are equal and are called to the same dignity and love. He does not prefer one population over another. If he has called the Jews, it is to show, that he calls all people. If he has shown his saving grace at a particular point in time, it is to show that he was saving people at all times. If Jerusalem is a holy sanctuary to meet God, Constantinople, Rome, New York, Beijing, Benares and the rest are also holy places to meet God. If God has manifested his love in his Son, then it is to show ineffably that he loves all as his children for, as Saint Paul revives the Old Testament teaching, 'For we are the temple of the living God! As God himself has said, 'I will make my home with my people and live among them; ... I will be your father and you shall be my sons and daughters, says the Lord Almighty.' All these promises are made to us, my dear friends.' (Second Corinthians 6:16-7:1) Or in Galatians 4: 4-5:

But when the right time finally came, God sent his own Son. He came as the son of a human mother and lived under the Jewish Law, to redeem those who were under the Law, so that we might become God's sons. To show that you are his sons, God sent the Spirit of his Son into our hearts, the Spirit who cries out, 'Father, my Father'. So then, you are no longer a slave but a son. And since you are his son, God will give you all that he has for his sons.

The unique Sonship of Jesus has meaning only with reference to the call God addresses to all men and women to enter into the intimate Father-son (daughter) relationship with him.

Christ's presence in the Eucharist is but a symbol
Finally, the *Explanatory Note* attributes an error to Father de Mello over his view on Eucharist being a mere symbol. The support for this accusation is taken from the author of *La Iluminacion*. It is one of those fantasies of the author of this mysterious Spanish text, which mixes up de Mello with Teilhard de Chardin and his mysticism of Eucharist. As I have noted in his biography, Father de Mello loved Eucharist, said Mass every day and concelebrated it whenever he had the opportunity. He meant there to celebrate the expression of faith and union with the Holy Roman Catholic Church. Those who attended his Mass or concelebrated with him had not the slightest suspicion or apprehension as to the authenticity of his faith. Let not Rome caste doubt on him twelve years after his death.

In conclusion to this discussion we can note that:
• The *Notification* does not make a global study of Father de Mello's Christ-centred spirituality but draws a superficial and sometimes faulty picture of his teachings.
• The Roman document does not show sensitivity to the problems involved in different dialogical situations like in India, or in the New Age and anti-Christian attitudes in the Occident, where a picture of Jesus Christ needs to be projected which is free from all imperial assumptions and superiority complexes. Christians are required to adopt a pedagogical approach beginning with the discovery of the person of Jesus, leading people gradually to an appreciation of his divinity.
• The document falsely accuses Father de Mello of reducing Jesus to the status of a master, one among many. He never indulged in such comparisons. His writings, when read in their context, cannot be interpreted in the sense of this reduction.
• The *Notification* confuses the spiritual sonship of Jesus Christ,

which Father de Mello taught, with the divine sonship in which he attests his firm faith.
• Again, the *Notification* bases its arguments on sources or on authors who have published their own misunderstandings, attributing them to Father de Mello.

16. FINAL DESTINY: DISSOLVING INTO THE IMPERSONAL GOD

NOTIFICATION
• In addition, the author's statements on the final destiny of men give rise to perplexity.

EXPLANATORY NOTE

• At one point, he speaks of a 'dissolving' into the impersonal God, as salt dissolves in water.

• Man's being seems destined to dissolve, like salt in water: 'Before that last bit dissolved, the [salt] doll exclaimed in wonder, 'Now I know who I am!'' (*The Song of the Bird*, 125).

In the so called 'New Age' circles one frequently comes across a teaching that holds the ultimate destiny of human beings like dissolution of the person into a mysterious, infinite mass, like a drop of water mingling with the boundless ocean. Teachings from Taoism, Hinduism and Buddhism are often cited in support of this position. Whether or not the Oriental religions do, in fact, support wishful New Age thinking is another matter. But many an Occidental theologians, theologising over a smattering of knowledge of Oriental religions have, in fact, widely propagated in the West such a biased opinion of Eastern religions.

What the Oriental masters like Sankara, Raamaanuja and Madhva teach with extremely delicate distinctions, about the relationship between man, the world and God, cannot be so easily discarded as a crude amalgam of the human into the divine. The misconceived, so-called New Age doctrines on salvation, can in no way be supported by an ill-presented oriental *advaita* ('non-duality') wrought with misunderstandings.

The Roman *Notification* seems to read such a New-Age doctrine in a humorous story, which is one among others compiled over the theme of ego. It has a lesson: the need to diminish and dissolve the ego on the path of the discovery of God. Moreover, a solitary story of this kind cannot be linked with any systematic teaching of Father de Mello about metaphysical or spiritual destiny of man conceived as a dissolution, much less a dissolution in an impersonal God. The *Notification* reads Father de Mello altogether out of context or reads him against the background of other positions untenable by Christian teachings and somehow draws him into heretical grounds which are totally foreign to him.

Let us first read the short story:
A salt doll journeyed for thousands
of miles over land, until it finally came to the sea.
It was fascinated by this strange moving mass,
quite unlike like anything it had ever seen before.
'Who are you?' said the salt doll to the sea.
The sea smilingly replied, 'Come in and see.'
So the doll waded into the sea. The further it walked into the sea the more it dissolved until there was only little of it left. Before that last bit dissolved, the doll exclaimed in wonder, 'Now I know who I am!'
(*The Song of the Bird*, 124-125)

Neither this story nor Father de Mello's other writings deal with terms like the 'impersonal God' as we have noted above when we treated de Mello's concept of God. On the contrary, his teachings are always a strong and consistent plea for an intimate personal experience of God. The context of this story in particular seems to be very personal, a personal dialogue between the elements: the lake, the ocean and the salt doll. It seems a bit exaggerated to me to solemnly conclude from this story and on the Christian doctrinal level, as does the Vatican document, that 'Man's being seems destined to dissolve, like salt into water.'

What Father de Mello tries to illustrate in this story is the experience that a person undergoes on the spiritual path: the dissolution of Ego before the awakening to the Self takes place. This is the ancient Oriental teaching which, however strange it might appear, is also the fundamental Christian spiritual teaching if one correctly understands what one means by 'Ego' and 'dissolution.' It is not the dissolution of the individual person, as many Christians fear to think, that is, losing one's own identity in the mass of an indefinable whole. What the Christian as well as the Oriental masters mean by 'ego' is the illusory idea that a person has of oneself; an idea formed through years of life on earth by identifying oneself with transitory things, in their appropriation or rejection. Oriental as well as Christian spirituality make this ego-dissolution an absolute condition in order to come to God.

The West and also Christianity seem to have great difficulties in correctly evaluating the Oriental teachings on ego and its suppression or dissolution. The psychological teachings in the West often tend to identify the individual person with his ego-achievements; whereas in Eastern psychology and spirituality, the true identity of the person is seen not in the transient identity of the ego (*ahamkara*) but of the Self (*atman*). 'Ego' is only the practical idea that man makes of himself through the vicissitudes of life and its history, limiting and defining himself through the different roles he plays in life and with which he identifies himself.

The expression 'dissolution of the ego' provokes fear among some Christians who are somewhat horrified by the thought of 'losing one's identity', the 'person' created in the likeness of God. They tend to think that, in spite of the reality of death, they carry their works and achievements into eternity. Popular Christian spirituality and our doctrine of merit do not dissipate such an idea of moving into paradise. That which we take into eternity is not the baggage of our deeds but that which the deeds have fashioned in us, until it, too, is rendered perfect through the Perfect Vision of God. In heaven, all will receive the 'highest pay'.

Father de Mello's teachings on the 'ego' and 'Self' are communicated primarily through stories. The story of Jitoku (*The Prayer of the Frog I*, 234) is a candid illustration of the former. This famous poet decided to become a Zen monk. His master welcomed him into the monastery with a slap firmly administered on his cheek before the gazing look of a throng that had gathered to witness the entry of the worldly man into religious life. Offended, he decided to challenge the master to a duel but then changed his mind when a disciple advised him to take the slap as a gesture of love and start meditating over it. Three days and nights of intense meditation then lead into the delightful *satori* or 'enlightenment' confirmed by the master. The slap was indeed a gesture of love: it had uprooted and dissolved his ego.

Another story illustrates the same teaching:

A man came to Buddha with an offering of flowers in his hands. Buddha looked up at him and said, 'Drop it!'

He couldn't believe he was being asked to drop the flowers. But then it occurred to him that he was probably being invited to drop the flowers he had in his left hand, since to offer something with one's left hand was considered inauspicious and impolite. So he dropped the flowers that his left hand held.

Still Buddha said: 'Drop it!'

This time he dropped all the flowers and stood empty-handed before Buddha who once again said, with a smile, 'Drop it!'

Perplexed, the man asked, 'What is it I am supposed to drop?'

'Not the flowers, son, but the one who brought them,' was Buddha's reply.

(*The Prayer of the Frog I*, 195-196)

The Self and the Subject cannot be defined nor grasped as an object. People identify it inadequately with their profession, activities or religion. The story of the woman in a coma brought before the Judgement Seat is probably the best illustration of the ego:

'Who are you?' asked an unseen voice.

'I am the wife of the mayor.' She replied.

'I did not ask you whose wife you are but who you are.'

'I'm the mother of four children.'

'I did not ask whose mother you are, but who you are.'

'I'm a schoolteacher.'

'I did not ask you what your profession is but who you are.'

And so it went. No matter what she replied, she did not seem to give an satisfactory answer to the question, 'Who are you?'

'I'm a Christian.'

'I did not ask what your religion is but who you are.'

'I'm the one who went to church every day and always helped the poor and needy.'
'I did not ask you what you did but who you are.'
She evidently failed the examination for she was sent back to earth. When she recovered from her illness she was determined to find out who she was. And that made all the difference.
(*The Prayer of the Frog I*, 191-192)

The question then becomes acute: who am I? What is my true identity? Father de Mello does not give a ready made answer to this question but, instead, tells the following enigmatic story, which is a Sufi tale:

The lover knocked at th door of his Beloved.
'Who knocks?' said the Beloved from within.
'It is I,' said the lover.
'Then go away. This house will not hold you and me.'
The rejected lover went away into the desert.
There he meditated for months on end, pondering the words of the Beloved. Finally he returned and knocked at the door again.
'Who knocks?'
'It is you.'
The door immediately opened.
(The Song of the Bird, 126-127)

The Sufis tell this tale to show that there is no place for 'I' or 'you' before God. One knows how 'I' often becomes an unbearable burden in human relationships when one tries to impose oneself on the other. Such an 'I' is meaningless before God. On the contrary, there is immense place for 'you' in a relationship. No relationship is stifled with the consciousness of 'you'. Isn't that precisely what Christians call the beatific vision in which the 'I' will be seen through the eternal 'you' as St Paul attests: 'Now I know in part; then I shall understand fully, even as I have been fully understood.' (1 Cor 13:12)

The dissolution of the ego is the suppression of the selfish pride of the individual person who is ignorant of his true self. In the Christian tradition the practice of renunciation and asceticism are based on that presumption. Spirituality is therefore the way of life that is centred not on the ego but on the true Self-identity of the person. For a Christian this identity is acquired through baptism in the name of Jesus Christ. As the apostle Paul says: 'But you are not in the flesh, you are in the Spirit, if in fact the Spirit of God dwells in you. Any one who does not have the Spirit of Christ does not belong to him.' (Romans 8:9) It must be noted that Christianity has not developed in this field of ego-Self a consistently clear distinction and discernment applicable in spiritual life. Its teaching can be sometimes ambiguous, when the spiritual strivings become an indirect pampering of the ego rather than its destruction. Spiritual guides do not always clearly advise their clients to try to pull down their illusory identity. Conversely, they sometimes adulate it through praise and consoling exhortations to bear with the sufferings provoked by this ego and make a sacred oblation of it. It would be more efficacious to clearly advice them to tear it down and show the concrete way to do it, as does Father de Mello in his teachings.

Going back to the story of the salt doll, one can note that the initial question that the doll puts to the ocean is 'Who are you?' The answer comes only at the end when the doll discovers its own true self: 'Now I know who I am.' When one's eyes are opened to God and when one sees him face to face, the feeling resulting from this extraordinary experience is the sense of one's own smallness and nothingness. The pretentious little salt doll comes to understand its true nature: the ocean. Has the salt doll lost its identity by dissolving itself into the ocean, or has it discovered its true identity?

17. Time and Destiny after Death

NOTIFICATION

• On various occasions, the question of destiny after death is declared to be irrelevant; only the present life should be of interest.

EXPLANATORY NOTE

• At other times, the question of life after death is declared to be unimportant: 'But is there life after death or is there not?' persisted a disciple. 'Is there life before death? – that is the question!' said the Master enigmatically.' (*One Minute Wisdom*, 83; cf ibid, 26).

• 'One sign that you're awakened is that you don't give a damn about what's going to happen in the next life. You're not bothered about it; you don't care. You are not interested, period.' (*Awareness*, 42-43, 150).

• Perhaps with even greater clarity: 'Why bother about tomorrow? Is there a life after death? Will I survive after death? Why bother about tomorrow? Get into today.' (*Awareness*, 114). 'The idea that people have of eternity is stupid. They think that it will last forever because it is outside of time. Eternal life is now; it's here.' (*La iluminación es la espiritualidad*, 42).

The *Explanatory Note* seems to say that Father de Mello denies, or at least deems irrelevant, the question of life after death, insisting only on life in the present. His teachings are therefore seen as a sort of materialistic doctrine, as if there was nothing after death or at least that one was unsure about it. This is a grotesque misunderstanding of Father de Mello's spirituality. It is true that he did not discuss life after death in the traditional Christian eschatological terms like 'the last judgement,' 'the retribution,' 'heaven' or 'hell'. Such themes were not really the problems of his religious audience, although some had serious difficulties integrating them in their spiritual life. What de Mello's listeners needed, in fact, was liberation from fear in life and fear for life. They needed help to come realise the great gift of God, which is life here and now. De Mello was more interested in showing people how to cherish the present and not waste it on account of the fear of the past or of the future. Some of the religious people who came to him were, in fact, tortured by the idea of death and eternal damnation to such an extent that they had unconsciously stopped living. It was important to remind them of the words of Jesus: 'Look at the birds of the air: they neither sow nor reap nor gather into barns, and yet your heavenly Father feeds them. Are you not of more value than they?' (Matthew 6:26) or 'For what will it profit a man if he gains the whole world and forfeits his life?' (Matthew 16:26). On this latter text the reader may consult a splendid meditation of Father de Mello in the opening chapter in his book *Call to Love*.

The teachings of Father de Mello on life after death have to be seen also against the background of another audience: his Occidental audience which, paradoxically is manifestly more preoccupied with the idea of reincarnation than persons in the Hindu and Buddhist countries. The past and the future, death and life after death, and the human destiny ruled by the blind law of karma seem to seize the mind and heart of many in the modern West. One knows through various polls conducted in the recent years that more than 25% of the Western population believes in reincarnation or has a tendency toward such beliefs. De Mello, therefore, felt it was important to remind such an audience in Europe and America that living now was more important than a fearful preoccupation with the future and with life after death.

The thought of death is nonetheless a painful reality to face. The sudden end it brings to life, severing it from its possessions and its unfulfilled desires and projects, can be a trauma. Human beings have always put the question: what is the meaning of death? Father de Mello in his answer to this enigmatic question not only tries to bring out the beauty of death but points out that true death is not the end of the biological process of life but the incapacity to live and enjoy life when one has all the chances and means for it. People seem to prefer to be dead when so much life vibrates around them. So goes his story:

'Some people claim there is no life after death,' said a disciple.
'Do they?' said the Master non-committally.
'Wouldn't it be awful to die – and never again see or hear or love or move?'
'You find that awful?' said the Master. 'But that's how most people are before they die.'
(*One Minute Nonsense*, 200)

The objection raised by the *Explanatory Note* belongs to one such story in which Tony de Mello contrasts moments of life with preoccupation with death filled with anguish:

All questions at the public meeting that day were about life beyond the grave.
The Master only laughed and did not give a single answer.
To his disciples, who demanded to know the reason for his evasiveness, he later said, 'Have you observed that it is precisely those who do not know what to do with this life who want another that will last forever?'
'But is there life after death or is there not?' persisted a disciple.
'Is there life before death? – that is the question!' said the Master enigmatically.
(*One Minute Wisdom*, 83)

The important sentence in this story is 'Have you observed that it is precisely those who do not know what to do with this life who want another that will last forever?' This sentence is not to be applied to those who live in the present in the hope of the Resurrection. Father de Mello on the contrary focuses on people who are restlessly preoccupied with the future life, or rather, future lives, reincarnations, karma and the rest. He wants to teach them that life in the here and now is more important than what might come after death or the number of lives that one may have to go through after death. Furthermore, the second reference to page 26 is wrong. Probably the *Explanatory Note* means page 122, where we read that heaven is here and now:

> To a disciple who was obsessed with the thought of life after death, the Master said, 'Why waste a single moment thinking of the hereafter?'
> 'But is it possible not to?'
> 'Yes.'
> 'How?'
> 'By living in heaven here and now.'
> 'And where is this heaven?'
> 'It is here and now.'
> (*One Minute Wisdom*, 122)

It might be appropriate at this point to recall that, according to Christian teachings, heaven and hell are not places but states. It is a state in which man is here and now, in heaven or in hell. However, having said that, the teachings in the Bible and in the tradition of the church do depict heaven and hell in glorious and ghastly imagery that evoke in the conscience of Christians images of luminous or horrendous *places* rather than an experience of states. Christian teaching on eschatology is still in its beginnings. We have difficulty in explaining heaven, hell and eternity. Could heaven and hell be the here and now, as in the words of Jesus speaking of the kingdom? What is eternity where there is no space and time? Isn't eternity here and now?

The next quote from *Awareness* cited by the *Explanatory Note* is again out of context: 'One sign that you're awakened is that you don't give a damn about what's going to happen in the next life. You're not bothered about it; you don't care. You are not interested, period.' (*Awareness*, 42-43, 150). Father de Mello does not want to brush aside the discussion about life after death but, instead, wants to give the right perspective to it. He says:

> The great mystics and masters in the East will say, 'Who are *you*?' Many think the most important question in the world is: 'Who is Jesus Christ?' Wrong! Many think it is: 'Does God exist?' Wrong! Nobody seems to be grappling with the problem of: Is there a life *before* death? Yet my experience is that it's precisely the ones who don't know what to do with this life who are all hot and bothered about what they are going

> to do with another life. One sign that you are awakened is that you don't give a damn about what's going to happen in the next life. You are not bothered about it; you don't care. You are not interested.
> (*Awareness*, 42-43)

Read in the right context, the quoted phrase will not bear insinuating and sinister shades of interpretation. It is simply healthy and Christian, as can be seen in the lives of so many of the awakened saints, engrossed as they are in the present, not to be bothered with life after death.

The reference to page 150 given by the *Explanatory Note* further points out the right perspective in which death has to be seen. Here again, Christian spirituality rarely speaks of a state of awakening in the present, since the general tendency is to stress 'heaven after death'. But the New Testament teaching –particularly its concept of the kingdom or reign of God – is both now and the future. The future is the continuation of what is taking place here and now. The kingdom of God is among us; it grows into its fullness in the future. The church is precisely this communion in the here and now of those who celebrate their salvation (and their heaven?) as they march towards the fullness in Christ Jesus. This is what Father de Mello says:

> Death is not a tragedy at all. Dying is wonderful; it's only horrible to people who have never understood life. It's only when you are afraid of life that you fear death. It's only dead people who fear death. But people who are alive have no fear of death. One of your American authors put it so well. He said that awakening is the death of your belief in injustice and tragedy. The end of the world for a caterpillar is a butterfly for the master. Death is resurrection. We're talking not about some resurrection that will happen but about one that is happening right now. If you would die to the past, if you would die to every minute, you would be the person who is fully alive, because a fully alive person is one who is full of death. We're always dying to things. We're always shedding everything in order to be fully alive and to be resurrected at every moment. The mystics, saints, and others make great efforts to wake people up. If they don't wake up, they're al-

ways going to have these other minor ills like hunger, wars, and violence. The greatest evil is sleeping people, ignorant people.
(*Awareness*, 150-151)

Anxiety and fear are signs of suffering and not of hope. Those who live are freed from fear. Anxiety is the sign of death, that you are not living in the present. Anxiety goes against the teaching of the gospels:

> So why are you anxious? Can you, for all your anxieties, add a single moment to your life? Why bother about tomorrow? Is there a life after death? Will I survive after death? Why bother about tomorrow? Get into today. Someone said, 'Life is something that happens to us while we're busy making other plans.' That's pathetic. Live in the present moment. This is one of the things you will notice happening to you as you come awake. You find yourself living in the present, tasting every moment as you live it. Another fairly good sign is when you hear the symphony one note after the other without wanting to stop it.
> (*Awareness*, 114)

As I have already pointed out above in the chapter two, Father de Mello brings in here a concept of time that is in the perspectives of Eastern religions. In Christianity, time is a continuum of past, present and future. Christianity gives equal, if not more, importance to the past and future in comparison to the present. Our past, ridden with sin, needs to be cleansed and pardoned. People sometimes stress it more than the saving grace and life that God gifts us in the present. Very often, we do not pay enough heed to the present, which seems to be only a fleeting moment. Hinduism and Buddhism consider the continuum of time (past, present and future) a phenomenon of illusion (*maayaa*) or of ignorance (*avidyaa*). What they say thereby is that the only reality is the present, because it is only the present that truly exists in itself, independently of our mind. The whole past and the whole future are only reminiscences or projections in the mind. They do not exist anywhere as such independently of mind. Our consciousness can open to this reality and recognise it. The past compared to the present is dead. It does not exist, except that it can only linger on in the spirit as memory. It would be, therefore, a gruesome illusion or ignorance to ignore the present reality on account of the past or the unknown future; an abominable loss to barter the living present with the dead past.

The Eastern religions and philosophies do not thereby in any way belittle or seem to neglect the past or the future. They are fully aware of the power of this *maayaa* that is past or the future. Although dead realities, they can powerfully influence the present through the memories, positive or negative, they leave in the consciousness. The memory of a good deed can positively influence and better the present; similarly, the negative and evil frames of mind created by the past can prevent the person from approaching the present with an open and healthy mind. If the person is not aware of this past lingering in the mind, it is likely that he or she repeats it in the future.

The meaning of the whole past or of the future lies, in fact, only in its capacity to prepare the consciousness of a person for the present. The past or the future that cuts one off from the present is of no use: it is harmful, for it wastes God's gift of life and grace revealed in the reality of life that is the present.

Here precisely lies the meaning of eternity. In Christian spirituality, eternity is very often pictured as something that 'lasts for ever'. However, eternity does not 'last'. The duration is only a concept linked to matter and to its quality of extension in space. It is the movement in space that marks time. A state in which there is no matter can also have no duration and time. Eternity is the fullness of the present. When the barriers of past and future fall, then one is left with the present in its totality, which is eternity. In the here and now, one does not have – or perhaps one has not developed – faculties to grasp this totality of the present, the art and knowledge to prescind from the past and from the future. Death probably makes one sink into the timeless state. In any case, the vision of God face-to-face is precisely that. It draws away all limitations set by the conscience. The consciousness contemplating God is the Consciousness of God contemplating us: 'For now we see through a glass, darkly; but then face to face: now I know in part; but then shall I know even as also I am known.' (1 Cor 13:12)

In the here and now, one can have only a fleeting inkling of this eternity in moments of intense love, compassion or joy; in mystical states or when God's grace touches our hearts. Or even in moments of artistic ecstasy, when the spirit is lifted up in grace and wonder.

We conclude by noting that the *Notification* reads Father de Mello partially and out of context. It does not try to see the perspectives in which de Mello spoke and taught about life after death. Therefore, it ends up drawing insinuating and unjust conclusions. It is not open to other perspectives brought in from other religions and spiritual sources, which could enrich the Christian vision of time and eternity.

18. Evil, Ethics and Morality; Sin and Repentance

NOTIFICATION

- With respect to this life, since evil is simply ignorance, there are no objective rules of morality.

- Good and evil are simply mental evaluations imposed upon reality.

EXPLANATORY NOTE

- Evil is nothing but ignorance, the lack of enlightenment: 'When Jesus looks at evil he calls it by its name and condemns it unambiguously. Only, where I see malice, he sees ignorance ... 'Father forgive them, for they do not know what they are doing.' [a]Lk 23:34, (*Wellsprings*, 215)

- Certainly, this text does not reflect the entire teaching of Jesus on the evil of the world and on sin; Jesus welcomed sinners with profound mercy, but he did not deny their sin; rather he invited them to conversion. In other passages we find even more radical statements: 'Nothing is good or bad but thinking makes it so.' (*One Minute Wisdom*, 104)

- 'Actually there is no good or evil in persons or in nature. There is only a mental judgement im-

posed upon this or that reality.'
(*Walking on Water*, 99)

• There is no reason to repent for sins, since the only thing that matters is to be awakened to an awareness of reality: 'Don't weep for your sins. Why weep for sins that you committed when you were asleep?' (*Awareness*, 26; cf ibid, 43, 150)

• The cause of evil is ignorance. (*One Minute Nonsense*, 239). Sin exists, but it is an act of insanity. (*La iluminación es la espiritualidad*, 63).

• Repentance therefore means returning to reality. (cf ibid, 48) 'Repentance is a change of mind: a radically different vision of reality.' (*One Minute Nonsense*, 241)

Father Anthony de Mello did not develop any particular formal position in his teaching or writings on the topic of morals or ethics. Neither his personal choice in his spiritual work nor the demands of his audience brought him to take positions on matters concerning ethics and morality. Nevertheless the *Explanatory Note* attributes to Father de Mello a position in which he is made responsible for having held that evil is nothing but ignorance. The context of the quote is Father de Mello's meditation on a gospel text (*Wellsprings*, 215). It is not so much a discourse on morality or ethics as the description of an attitude that can be adopted in education, or more precisely, the way of looking at things as an art in educating the hearts of people:

The gospels tell how Jesus turned and looked at Peter and how that look changed Peter's heart. (Matthew 26:75)
If Jesus were to come back to the world today, what would he look at first? ...
I imagine that what first attracts his notice is the overwhelm-

ing goodness in humanity. The good-hearted person sees goodness everywhere; the evil-hearted evil, for we tend to see in others the reflection of ourselves. Jesus uncovers by his look the love, the honesty and goodness that hides in every human being. I see him looking at a prostitute ... then I look at her as he does to discover what he sees in her ... I see him look at hardened tax-collectors ... at an adulterous woman ... at a thief on a cross beside him ... and I learn the art of looking!
When Jesus looks at evil he calls it by its name and condemns it unambiguously.
Only, where I see malice, he sees ignorance.
At the moment of his death I see him drop his anger at the Pharisees; he looks beyond their seeming malice:
'Father, forgive them, for they do not know what they are doing.' I take my time to look and listen, for it will educate my heart.
(*Wellsprings*, 213-215)

When seen in this context, it becomes clear that Father de Mello's teaching does not say that evil is nothing but ignorance but that 'where I see malice, Jesus sees ignorance and that's why he says 'Father forgives them ...' That is precisely Jesus' way of looking at things with his eyes of mercy and compassion. The way Jesus looks at men is not comparable to the looks of human beings that cast condemning glances at culprits. Jesus' look is the saving look that heals the heart of the sinner. What Jesus sees is not malice but the inability of the person to see things: his ignorance. This way of understanding the attitude of Jesus is in no way tp condone sin or evil, but to marvel at the infinite knowledge and compassion which looks beyond malice.

The Vatican authorities then make a methodological observation: 'This text does not reflect the entire teaching of Jesus on the evil of the world and on sin.' I wish they applied the same methodology also to Father Anthony de Mello's writings by trying to see his entire teaching and not just take sentences from 'here and there' in order to sow doubt and confusion. Furthermore, Father de Mello does not belittle sin or conversion. In fact, as shall be presently seen, his whole approach is for a true conversion, that is, abandoning the life of attachments and coming to the freedom of detachment; to see the reality and not remain in illusion.

'Nothing is good or bad, but thinking makes it so,' underlines the Roman text. The reference is given to *One Minute Wisdom*, page 104. This citation is yet another small error, the exact reference being to page 105. Again, Father de Mello does not speak on evil or morality but on prejudice in our dealings in daily life. Let us first read the entire text:

> 'Nothing is good or bad but thinking makes it so.' The Master said.
>
> When asked to explain he said. 'A man cheerfully observed a religious fast seven days a week. His neighbour starved to death on the same diet.'
>
> (*One Minute Wisdom*, 105)

A person fasts cheerfully and perhaps attains his liberation, whereas another, rather disgruntled, fasts, but his attitude is that of seeing the fast as a torture. That is what leads him to death. Nothing is good or bad in itself; things are harmless in themselves. It's the way one looks at them that makes them good or bad. A further example: two wonderful persons stand before me; but my prejudiced mind puts quickly labels on them. I notice that one of them is a 'German'; and, so, I tend to see in him a Nazi; the other is an 'Arab'; so, he must be a terrorist! This act of labelling people is what Jesus condemned and fought against. In all cases, he gave importance to men and not the labels they carried.

Regarding the next quotation, 'Actually there is no good or evil in persons or in nature, there is only a mental judgement imposed upon this or that reality' (*Walking on water*, 99), the Roman writers go fishing for arguments by hook or by crook. Let us read the full text, although it is culled from a book whose authorship, as has been pointed out, is dubious:

> So we live with so many things filtered, selected, censored. What actually is there on our minds? We add to our images mental constructs and evaluations: 'This is good, this is bad, true, untrue, etc.' Actually there is no good or evil in persons or in nature. There is only a mental judgement imposed on

this or that reality: which team is good, which is best, when a victory is well earned, when the game isn't well played. In reality all that exists is a game and the people playing in it, a ball that is thrown, kicked, hurled. Ball and players move back and forth. People add their particular evaluations to these actions in life; they cheer more for a uniform or for an idea than for the reality that is already there. They applaud their own conditioning and preferences much more than the reality they observe. Isn't that stupid?
(*Walking on Water*, 99-100)

De Mello is describing here the psychological attitude that people take in life towards persons and things. Often what is seen as good or bad is not something that is in itself good or bad but the way one has been taught to look at it or the way one labels things in order to suit one's own attitude in life; that is what is called 'prejudice'. On prejudices, one builds one's life and life-goals. One does not meet people in order to discover and learn but to come back confirmed in one's prejudices regarding him or her. Even in simple and joyful things like a football match, one does not go to the game to enjoy it but to fight the other team, often even beyond the game. The enjoyment is linked only to the victory of 'my' team. If they do not win, then the whole time has been a big frustration. To illustrate this attitude in life, Father Anthony de Mello has an interesting tale of Jesus' going to a football match:

Jesus Christ said he had never been to a football match. So we took him to one, my friends and I. It was a ferocious battle between the Protestant Punchers and the Catholic Crusaders.
The Crusaders scored first. Jesus cheered wildly and threw his hat high up in the air. Then the Punchers scored. And Jesus cheered wildly and threw his hat high up in the air.
This seemed to puzzle the man behind us. He tapped Jesus on the shoulder and asked, 'Which side are you shouting for, my good man?'
'Me?' replied Jesus, by now visibly excited by the game. 'Oh! I'm not shouting for either side. I'm just here to enjoy the game.'
The questioner turned to his neighbour and sneered, 'Hmm, an atheist!'

On the way back we briefed Jesus on the religious situation of the world today. 'It's a funny thing about religious peoples, Lord,' we said, 'they always seem to think that God is on their side and against the people on the other side.'

Jesus agreed. 'That is why I don't back religions, I back people,' he said. 'People are more important than religions. Man is more important than the Sabbath.'

'You ought to watch your words,' one of us said with some concern, 'You were crucified once for saying that sort of thing, you know.' 'Yes – and by religious peoples,' said Jesus with a wry smile.

(*The Song of the Bird*, 190-191)

Things could be so wonderful and so enjoyable if one only knew the art of looking at them as they are and not through the prism of one's prejudices, one's craving appropriation.

There is an implicit critique here of an attitude, largely found among 'good' Christians who take to God in prayer their wishful desires to 'win', begging God to be gracious to their prayer. What God grants is not their fanciful demands but the strength to give up all attachments that create in us such desires, and to learn to see the gift of God in all things. The reader will be deliciously delighted if he or she reads the story of the restless devotee of Vishnu:

The Lord Vishnu was so tired of his devotee's constant petitions that he appeared to him one day and said: 'I have decided to grant you any three things you ask for. After that, I shall give you nothing more.'

The devotee delightedly made his first petition at once. He asked that his wife should die so that he could marry a better woman. His petition was immediately granted.

But when friends and relatives gathered for the funeral and began to recall all the good qualities of his wife, the devotee realised he had been hasty. He now realised he had been quite blind to all her virtues. Was he likely to find another woman quite as good as her?

So he asked the Lord to bring her back to life!

That left him with just one petition. And he was determined not to make a mistake this time, for he would have no chance to correct it.

THE NOTIFICATION

He consulted widely. Some of his friends advised him to ask for immortality. But of what good was immortality, said others, if he did not have good health? And of what use was health if he had no money? And of what use was money if he had no friends?

Years passed and he could not make up his mind what to ask for: life or health or wealth or power or love. Finally he said to the Lord, 'Please advise me on what to ask for.'

The Lord laughed when he saw the man's predicament, and said, 'Ask to be contented no matter what life brings you.'
(*The Song of the Bird*, 184-85)

The statement of the *Explanatory Note* concluding that 'there is no reason to repent for sins ...' is a misunderstanding of de Mello, who makes a sharp distinction between 'Don't weep for your sins' and 'repent'. Weeping for sins is, for de Mello, an act of closing in upon oneself, whereas repentance is opening to the mercy and love of God. As has been noted just above, sin, repentance and conversion are major recurring themes in Father de Mello's teachings. However, de Mello stresses more the 'change of heart or mind' (*metanoia*) than the attitude of self-punishment as satisfaction. Let one first place the text cited in its context:

Imagine a stage magician who hypnotises someone so that the person sees what is not there and does not see what is there. That's what it's all about. Repent and accept the good news. Repent! Wake up! Don't weep for your sins. Why weep for your sins that you committed when you were asleep? Are you going to cry because of what you did in your hypnotised state? Why do you want to identify with a person like this? Wake up! Wake up! Repent! Put on a new mind. Take on a new way of looking at things!
(*Awareness*, 26)

It is quite clear that Father de Mello invites people to repent, to put on a new mind, to look at things anew and not just brood over the sins committed. I cannot see how the Roman document can conclude from this text that 'there is no reason to repent for sin'. On this there is more to read in Father de Mello:

People are so distressed when I tell them to forget their past. They are so proud of their past. Or they are so ashamed of

their past. They're crazy? Just drop it! When you hear 'Repent for your past,' realise it's a great religious distraction from waking up. Wake up! That's what repent means. Not 'Weep for your sins.' Wake up! Understand, stop all crying. Understand! Wake up!
(*Awareness*, 43)

If you would die to the past, if you would die to every minute, you would be the person who is fully alive, because a fully alive persons is one who is full of death.
(*Awareness*, 150-151)

To understand this teaching and in order to correctly evaluate it, one has to be aware of the spiritual concept of time which I have tried to describe above. The past as such has not existence except in the minds and memories of people. It does not exist in itself as the present exists. The present is something to which I open my eyes, I become aware of. It is there, independently of my mind. This focus on the present, however, does not mean that the past is unimportant and not to be accounted for or that one has no responsibility towards it. The past in fact is very active, often more active in our conscience and consciousness than the present. Even if it is dead in its nature, the past is alive through the film that it leaves on our spirit through which we perceive the present. It has no existence as such, but it is active. It is not by weeping continuously over the past that one can free oneself from it but by opening one's mind and heart to the present.

However, one knows that there is a Christian spirituality, one which the Roman authors probably share, that understands repentance as weeping over one's sins. One can weep and torture oneself for sins. I remember how a pious Jesuit spiritual Father used to extol in his exhortations models of sanctity. His favourite example was Saint Francis Borgia, an offshoot of the notorious Borgia family, and one of the first Jesuit Superior Generals. This saint used to torture his body by intense flagellation, and confess his past sins daily, even twice a day. This self torture is not sanctity but an insane brutality towards one's own Ego. Thereby one fosters it all the more through torture, subtly covering it with the mantle of a so-called sanctity. Ultimately, what is important is not our sins, but the pardon and the grace of

God. Furthermore, this pardon is not a thing of the past but the gracious reality of the present, because God is a living God who grants pardon in the here and now. One has to open one's heart and mind to him here and now in the present. This opening is what Jesus teaches when he says that the shepherd goes after the lost sheep leaving the ninety-nine others behind: 'And if he finds it, truly, I say to you, he rejoices over it more than over the ninety-nine that never went astray.' (Matthew 18:13)

Elsewhere in *Sadhana – A Way to God*, Father de Mello has a splendid teaching regarding repentance, which has not been noticed by the Roman survey. It is a teaching that might appear strange to pious Catholics but which is Christian in its depths. It is thanking God for having permitted one to commit sins! How strange to thank God for the abominable acts committed instead of weeping, smearing oneself with ashes and gnashing one's teeth. Let us read Father de Mello:

> Sin is obviously something that we must hate and avoid. Yet we can praise God even for our sins when we have repented for them, because he will draw great good from them. And so the church, in an ecstasy of love, will sing at the Easter liturgy, 'O happy fault ... O necessary sin of Adam!' And St Paul explicitly tells the Romans, 'Where sin increased, God's grace increased much more ... what shall we say, then? That we should continue to live in sin so that God's grace will increase? Certainly not!' (Romans 5:20, 6:1)
> This is something we hardly think of: to think and praise God even for our sins! It is right that we regret our sins. But, having done this, we must also learn to praise God for them.
> (*Sadhana – A Way to God,* 131-132)

Father de Mello then gives a concrete method of prayer into which one can enter with praise and thanksgiving:

> Try this yourself now:
> Think of something in the past or present that is causing you pain or distress or frustration ...
> If you are in any way to blame for this thing express your regret and sorrow to the Lord ...
> Now explicitly thank God for this, praise him for it ... Tell him that you believe that even this fits into his plan for you

and for others, even though you may not see the good ...
(*Sadhana – A Way to God*, 132)

This is the meaning of repentance. Repentance is not castigating oneself on account of one's past sins and weeping for them but opening the heart in thanksgiving to God for his mercy showered on us. Because of the experience of sin, one can now avoid it and do good instead. Instead of wasting one's time and energy by breeding guilt feelings and torturing oneself (and perhaps torturing others, too), one can opens one's heart in thanksgiving.

'Sin exists, but it is an act of insanity.' This phrase is again from *La iluminación es la espiritualidad*. The final remarks, 'repentance therefore means returning to reality' and 'repentance is a change of mind, a radically different vision of reality,' should not be objectionable in any way to the Catholic faith. I do not see why the *Notification* finds fault with this teaching. Isn't this change of mind what the New Testament calls *metanoia*, repentance (Matthew 3:2)? The context will give us the correct perspective for understanding this new mind:

'Why do you never teach repentance?' said the preacher.
'It's the only thing I teach,' said the Master.
'But I never hear you speak on sorrow for sin.'
'Repentance isn't sorrow for the past. The past is dead and isn't worth a moment's grief. Repentance is a change of mind: a radically different vision of reality'.
(*One Minute Nonsense*, 241)

The Roman text from now on manifests a malicious tone. Statements that are made against Father de Mello take the form of false accusations. His words are twisted and placed out of context; distorted in order to make an argument of them. To come to the conclusion that de Mello says that evil is simply ignorance, as the *Notification* does, that there are no objective rules of morality, and that good and evil are simply mental evaluations imposed upon reality, are grotesque distortions of Father de Mello's ideas. 'Evil is nothing but ignorance, the lack of enlightenment' are not Father de Mello's words but the hasty and distorted conclusion of the *Notification*. As has been pointed out in this study, all the texts quoted by the *Notification* in proof of Father de Mello's so called fallacies are examples of misunderstandings and misinterpretations, implying sometimes a wanton will to degrade the personality of Father de Mello and his teachings.

19. CHURCH HAS LOST THE AUTHORITY TO TEACH

NOTIFICATION

EXPLANATORY NOTE
(*Note:* In the official text the following paragraph comes before the above mentioned paragraph on evil, ethics and morality. I have brought it here to show its correspondence with the text of the *Notification* .)

- Consistent with what has been presented, one can understand how, according to the author, any belief or profession of faith whether in God or in Christ cannot but impede one's personal access to truth.

- At various points in his books institutions of the Church are criticized indiscriminately: 'My religious life has been completely taken over by professionals.' (*The Song of the Bird*, 63ff)

- The Church, making the word of God in Holy Scripture into an idol, has ended up banishing God from the temple.

- The function of the Creed or the Profession of the Faith is judged negatively, as that which prevents personal access to truth and enlightenment. (thus with different nuances, *The Song of the Bird* , 36, 46-47, 50ff, 215)

- She has consequently lost the authority to teach in the name of Christ.

- 'When you no longer need to hold on to the words of the Bible, it is then that it will become something very beautiful for you, revealing life and its message. The sad thing is that the official Church has dedicated itself to framing the idol, enclosing it,

> defending it, reifying it without being able to look at what it really means.' (*La iluminación es la espiritualidad*, 66).

> • Similar ideas are presented in *The Prayer of the Frog I*, 7, 94, 95, 98-99: 'A public sinner was excommunicated and forbidden entry to the church. He took his woes to God. 'They won't let me in, Lord, because I am sinner.' 'What are you complaining about?' said God. 'They won't let me in either!' (ibid.105)

It is astonishing to see how the *coup de grace* is given to the Jesuit who, through his very vows, was trained to think with the church, to love her 'as his own mother', fight for her and defend her, all of which Anthony de Mello did wholeheartedly whenever the occasion arose. He was a person loved by the church in India and elsewhere and was never heard belittling or mocking the church in his discourses or teachings, be they private or public. However, both the *Notification* and the *Explanatory Note* paint him as an enemy of the church. For those of us who knew Father de Mello personally, the description is shocking.

In the first citation concerning the professionals, Father de Mello does not mock the authorities of the church, but the context clearly shows that he speaks of the dry, routine life of certain religious people. We have seen elsewhere how he was trying in his spiritual guidance to bring people to experience direct contact with God and make the whole life's experience a continuous prayer by showing them imaginative ways and means to combat a dry routine in their spiritual life. The story illustrates the dry professionalism which can sometimes, even in our church, become part of one's spiritual life:

A native king in the South Pacific islands was giving a banquet in honour of a distinguished guest for the West.
When the time came to praise the guest, His Majesty re-

mained squatting on the floor while a professional orator, especially engaged for this purpose, laid it on thick.

After the eloquent panegyric, the guest rose to say a few words of thanks to the King. His Majesty gently held him back.

'Don't stand up,' he said. 'I have engaged an orator for you too. In our island we don't believe that public speaking should be engaged by amateurs.'

I wonder, would God appreciate it if I became more amateur myself in my dealings with him?

(*The Song of the Bird*, 63)

People who are acquainted with the religious life in monasteries and in religious houses know how quickly a certain routine professionalism can replace the adventurous spiritual experiment. Again, many a religious activity, like the reading of the Holy Hours, a Mass said in private, or the community prayers recited daily, can become simply a routine, meaningless task in the life of the religious. With time, some begin to worship formulas instead of reliving their content:

The mystic was back from the desert. 'Tell us,' they avidly said, 'What is God like?'

But how could he ever put into words what he had experienced in the depths of his heart? Is it possible to put truth into words?

He finally gave them a formula – so inaccurate, so inadequate – in the hope that some of them might be tempted, through it, to experience for themselves what he had experienced.

They seized upon the formula. They made a sacred text out of it. They imposed it upon everyone as a holy belief. They went to great pains to spread it in foreign lands. And some even gave their lives for it.

And the mystic was sad. It might have been better if he had never spoken.

(*The Song of the Bird*, 36)

The mystic is brought into contrast with the man of rituals. These attitudes can be found amply among religious people. Neither the story nor its lesson has anything to do with the creed or the profession of faith. The story of the devil and his friend cited by the *Explanatory Note* is a delicious story that has to be read as recounted by Father de Mello himself.

> The devil once went for a walk with a friend. They saw a man ahead of them stoop down and pick up something from the road.
> 'What did that man find?' asked the friend.
> 'A piece of Truth,' said the devil.
> 'Doesn't that disturb you?' asked the friend.
> 'No, it does not,' said the devil, 'I shall allow him to make a religious belief out of it.'
>
> A religious belief is a signpost pointing the way to Truth. People who cling tenaciously to the signpost, are prevented from moving towards the Truth because they have the false feeling that they already possess it.
> (*The Song of the Bird,* 46-47)

I wonder why the *Explanatory Note* misinterprets this story. It is a joke over religious beliefs which, instead of leading to the discovery and experience of truth, are made into objects of worship. Father de Mello never meant to say that one's creed or the profession of faith has been a work of converting truth into religious belief. It is one's way of reciting it – or blindly holding to its form and not to its content – that can sometimes take the style of professionals.

The next text alluded to comes out of de Mello's collection of stories concerning biblical interpretation. When Tony de Mello was studying theology, the biblical exegesis was done in Latin, even in India. The historical text-criticism was slowly making its way in biblical scholarship. But in India, as also elsewhere, it took a long time to read Genesis and other books of the Bible in the right perspectives of their literary styles. People used to be shocked when they were told that Genesis is not a historical book but a special literary genre and that one has not to take things there literally. People till then had, in fact, observed some internal difficulties if the text was interpreted literally. For example, God creates on the first day light and darkness; but the light that he creates has nothing to do with the sun, which is created only on the fourth day. Now, how come one talks of days –

the first, the second and so on – when the sun is created only on the fourth day? Well, the biblical teachers of the pre-Vatican II days said that everything was possible for God and, therefore, one had to take things as they were written. It's only later that we began to read Genesis a bit differently. The people whom Father de Mello mentions in the following story are those who treat biblical texts literally and to gave a literal meaning to the words they read:

> A Christian scholar who held the Bible to be literally true in every detail was once accosted by a colleague who said, 'According to the Bible the earth was created some five thousand years ago. But we have unearthed bones to show that life has existed on this planet for hundreds of thousands of years.'
> Pat came the scholar's answer: 'When God created the earth five thousand years ago, he deliberately planted those bones in the earth to see if we would give more credence to scientific assertions than to his Holy Word.'
> Further evidence of rigid belief leading to reality distortion.
> (*The Song of the Bird,* 50-51)

Clearly, Father de Mello has no intention of mocking religious truth or the institution of the church. He simply draws the attention of his hearers and readers to the need to go to the essential teaching of the word of God and not remain with words only.

The story of Simon Peter on page 214-215 is again a story about experiencing God and not an unpleasant joke on the church. How true it is that, in religious education, often ready-made answers are given to children before they can discover the truth for themselves. The Catholic catechisms and theological teachings often kill the innermost thirst people can have for God by producing ready-made categorical answers. De Mello illustrates through a story:

> *A dialogue from the gospels:*
> 'And you,' said Jesus, 'Who do you say I am?'
> Simon Peter answered, 'You are the Messiah, the Son of the living God.'
> Then Jesus said, 'Simon, son of Jonah, you are favoured indeed You did not learn that from mortal man: my heavenly Father revealed, it to you.'

A present-day dialogue:
Jesus:
'And you, who do you say I am?'
Christian:
'You are the Messiah, the Son of the living God.'
Jesus:
'Well and truly answered. But how unfortunate you are that you learnt this from mortal man. It has not yet been revealed to you by my heavenly Father.'
Christian:
'True, Lord. I have been cheated. Somebody gave me all the answers before your Heavenly Father could speak. I marvel at your own wisdom that you said nothing to Simon yourself, but waited for your Father to speak first.'
(*The Song of the Bird*, 214-215)

Take, for example, another of Tony's short stories that could have shocked the Roman authors had they noticed it:
When the guru sat down to worship each evening, the ashram cat would get in the way and distract the worshippers. So he ordered that the cat be tied during evening worship.
Long after the guru died the cat continued to be tied during evening worship. And when the cat eventually died, another cat was brought to the ashram so that it could be duly tied during evening worship.
Centuries later learned treatises were written by the guru's disciples on the essential role of a cat in all properly conducted worship.
(*The Song of the Bird*, 79)

Again, a very problematic quotation is cited from *La iluminación es la espiritualidad* p 66, on which I do not comment for the previously-stated reasons.

The stories to which the *Explanatory Note* alludes in the book, *The Prayer of the Frog*, are, again, illustrations of the direct experience of God which is questioned or the rigid attitudes of ritualism and of machine-like repetitive religious practices condemned by de Mello and are misunderstood. However, there is an important story to which allusion is made and which needs

THE NOTIFICATION

to be read in conclusion of this chapter for it illustrates not only Tony's role in the spiritual service but also the wily attitudes of his enemies:

> After many years of labour, an inventor discovered the art of making fire. He took his tools to the snow-clad northern regions and initiated a tribe into the art – and the advantages – of making fire. The people became so absorbed in this novelty that it did not occur to them to thank the inventor who one day quietly slipped away. Being one of those rare human beings endowed with greatness, he had no desire to be remembered or revered; all he sought was the satisfaction of knowing that someone had benefited from his discovery.
>
> The next tribe he went to was just as eager to learn as the first. But the local priests, jealous of the stranger's hold on the people, had him assassinated. To allay any suspicion of the crime, they had a portrait of the Great Inventor enthroned upon the main altar of the temple, and a liturgy designed so that his name would be revered and his memory kept alive. The greatest care was taken that not a single rubric of the liturgy was altered or omitted. The tools for making fire were enshrined within a casket and were said to bring healing to all who laid their hands on them with faith.
>
> The High Priest himself undertook the task of compiling a Life of the Inventor. This became the Holy Book in which his loving kindness was offered as an example for all to emulate, his glorious deeds were eulogised, his superhuman nature made an article of faith. The priests saw to it that the Book was handed down to future generations, while they authoritatively interpreted the meaning of his words and the significance of his holy life and death. And they ruthlessly punished with death or excommunication anyone who deviated from their doctrine. Caught up as they were in these religious tasks, the people completely forgot the art of making fire.
> (*The Prayer of the Frog I*, 7-8)

This story of the inventor of fire is an epitome of Father de Mello's life and what happened to him after his death. He is not the only victim. I think the prime victim was Jesus himself. And whosoever wants to perpetuate this art of fire-making seems to end up in the same way. It is easy and comfortable to venerate someone rather than live by his or her message.

The story on page ninety-four of the same book, alluded to in the Vatican text, (we have quoted it on page 148) is in fact a problematic story, particularly in India, where the success in missionary work was gauged by the number of conversions contributing to the increase of the Christian fold. One needs, however, to have an understanding of Father de Mello's sense of humour when he writes that Jesus would have applauded the loss of 500 people from the church membership. It's the revival within the church and the intensity with which the Christian message is lived that has reduced the size and not the neglect of the religious experience. The following stories on page ninety-five and the one after are, again, stories illustrating the hiatus between mystical experience and religious ritualism, both of which the *Explanatory Note* has taken amiss as criticisms of the church and its institutions.

Based on such a misunderstanding, the *Notification* makes a solemn affirmation regarding the supposed unorthodoxy of Father de Mello. However, one sentence seems to be particularly ignominious: 'The church, making a word of God in Holy Scripture into an idol has ended up banishing God from the temple. She has consequently lost the authority to teach in the name of Christ.' That is a pure construct of the Roman document, and such thoughts are to be found nowhere in the writings of Father de Mello. The *Notification* asserts this without giving a corresponding quotation from Father de Mello's writings in the *Explanatory Note*. I can write with certainty that such a sentence could not have come from his mouth, given the high love and esteem with which he held his allegiance to the Catholic Church and the respect with which the bishops in India esteemed his teachings, be they in sadhanas or retreats and conferences which he gave. The authors of the *Notification* here make a very unfortunate mistake by attributing to Father de Mello a false accusation for it has no passage from Father de Mello's writings to cite in the *Explanatory Note* to support its accusation. Based on some spurious writings, the Vatican authors have let themselves be misguided here.

Let us see in detail the quotations cited by the *Explanatory*

Note. It begins by saying, 'At various points in his books, institutions of the church are criticised indiscriminately.' However, in all of these quotations and elsewhere, Father de Mello never mentions the word 'church' nor makes directly or indirectly allusions to it. It is the writers of the *Notification* who see the church where de Mello has something else in mind. In fact, they see a fault where there is in fact not one. The three quotations taken from *The Song of the Bird* to illustrate that Father de Mello negatively judges the function of creed and the profession of faith are all out of context and based on biased judgements, as we have amply shown in previous cases.

ANTHONY DE MELLO

20. Danger

NOTIFICATION

• With the present *Notification*, in order to protect the good of the Christian faithful, this Congregation declares that the above-mentioned positions are incompatible with the Catholic faith and can cause grave harm.

EXPLANATORY NOTE

• Clearly, there is an internal connection between these different positions: if one questions the existence of a personal God, it does not make sense that God would address himself to us with his word. Sacred Scripture, therefore, does not have definitive value. Jesus is a teacher like others; only in the author's early books does he appear as the Son of God, an affirmation which would have little meaning in the context of such an understanding of God. As a consequence one cannot attribute value to the church's teaching. Our personal survival after death is problematic if God is not personal. Thus it becomes clear that such conceptions of God, Christ and man are not compatible with the Christian faith.

• For this reason, those responsible for safeguarding the doctrine of the faith have been obliged to illustrate the dangers in the texts written by Father Anthony de Mello or attributed to him, and to warn the faithful about them.

Summarising the document, the *Explanatory Note* mentions that there is 'an internal connection' between the objections raised. There is no doubt that there is an internal connection, but if the objections raised are unfounded, as I have tried to show, then the internal connection also becomes meaningless. This internal connection is nothing other than prejudices, based on rumours, against Father de Mello that have contributed to this Roman enquiry and its report. It is a strange way to go about criticising an author and is particularly unbecoming for the teaching authority of the church, who seems to be in this case witch-hunting in order to find reasons for a condemnation pronounced before hand.

I have tried to show an 'internal connection' in chapter two describing Father de Mello's spirituality. His approach begins with the interest he takes in making spirituality a healthy and happy experience of God. But he soon realises that what the Jesuits and people of other religious orders need, more than spirituality, is a healthy and happy life, healthy and happy in all its spheres. He takes up, therefore, the problems that religious face as barriers in the practice of spirituality. What are the effective means to pull down these barriers? His best tool is the Ignatian discernment – discerning attachment and detachment – whose meaning de Mello sees in depth also in other religions, notably in the Buddhist discernment of appropriation (*tanha*) and liberty (*nirvana*). For the Christian way of life, as de Mello develops, the discernment is to be seen concretely in the contemplation of life in Jesus Christ. The liberty to which Jesus calls is the liberty of the Children of God, the family of God on earth, the kingdom and the church. Seen this way, in admiration and love, Father de Mello's teaching is a tremendous help in coming to love God, the church and the whole of humanity through the example of the One whom he sent to humans as the Saviour and Redeemer.

The *Explanatory Note* gives its motivation as 'safeguarding the doctrine of the faith,' and the *Notification* wants what is best for 'the good of the Christian faithful.' I do not know if these goals have really been achieved by the Roman document. We will discuss this question further in the following chapter.

CHAPTER FOUR

Is Father Anthony de Mello a danger to the Catholic Faith?

The Vatican *Notification* concludes that some of the writings of Father de Mello are incompatible with the Catholic faith and, therefore, could be harmful or dangerous to the faithful. We have shown in our study in the previous chapter that all of the quotations adduced from Father de Mello's writings are misinterpreted or misquoted. Therefore, the *Notification* itself is unjust and unacceptable. The Vatican's warning needs to be further closely examined in the face of the reactions of people throughout the world, and particularly of those of the faithful in the Catholic Church. We know that the *sensus communis* plays an important role in the definition and interpretation of the teachings of the church. Does the church, which is spread all over the world, agree with the *Notification* and its conclusions?

Reactions to the Vatican Notification
In India, Father Anthony de Mello's home country, most people were dumbfounded to learn that the Vatican undertook to pinpoint one of their esteemed Jesuit priests, who was known to them as one doing good for a large number of people. The first reaction was denial. They thought that it simply could not be to him that the *Notification* refers and that there must be a mistake somewhere. People would have been less surprised if they had come to know that the Vatican had canonised this man of prayer and spirituality. There were, for sure, some religious men and women who had grievances against de Mello, offended as they might have been sometime or another by Tony's straightforward treatment.

Bishops and theologians in India knew that the Vatican, in recent years, was particularly hard on them. Ever since the publication of the encyclical *Redemptoris Missio*, it was known that

A DANGER TO THE CATHOLIC FAITH?

the officials of the Congregation for the Doctrine of the Faith and, to a certain extent, the Pope himself were disturbed by the newer theological interpretations developed by Indian theologians. Their thinking and expression sounded strange and foreign to Roman ears, attuned to Western language and tone. But de Mello was not a theologian and was never heard or seen in theological circles. He was a spiritual father to hundreds and thousands of people who had never felt or suspected anything amiss in his teachings. They were aware of Tony's humour and laughter on all matters, including sometimes the harmless but poignant remarks on church dignitaries and traditions. But his audience knew to sort out jokes from serious talk.

People looked to their pastors, the bishops, for a reaction.

Pastoral Guidelines of the bishops in India
The bishops in India took a clear and bold stand with regard to the Roman *Notification*. Without saying it in so many words, they have massively and unequivocally rejected it in its present form and content, defending the basic authenticity of Father de Mello's teachings.

The Pastoral Guidelines on the Writings of late Fr Tony de Mello (published by the Standing Committee of the Catholic Bishops' Conference of India, 1999) do not question the authority of the Congregation for the Doctrine of the Faith to intervene in matters of faith and order. Neither do they go to the extent, as ordered by Cardinal Ratzinger, of withdrawing Father Anthony de Mello's writings from the public. Several of the Indian bishops had known Father de Mello personally and had attended his conferences and retreats. They are bold witnesses to his authenticity and faith. Their guidelines point out the immense good that the man and his teachings have brought about for the church in India and for humanity at large. They promote a careful and critical reading of his writings, as good Christians should do with all writings, including the Bible.

The bishops point out that Father Tony wrote and taught in the context of the violence-ridden religious history of India. His teachings should be seen against the background of fanatical religious fundamentalism and communalism, which has caused hundreds of thousands of killings in God's name.

The bishops underline the aim of Father de Mello's writings:
> Trained spiritual director and psychological counsellor that he was, Fr Tony early on in his ministry realised that many priests, religious and educated laity were severely hampered in their pilgrim journey to communion with God, self and neighbour by innumerable emotional and psychological wounds. He was also keenly aware that immature faith and religious formalism also obstructed personal growth.
> (*Pastoral guidelines*, 2)

They add a very important note and a deep intuition to which the Vatican authorities were not sensitive:
> To those who did not really know this complex, compassionate person nor appreciate his pastoral purpose, his technique and pedagogical method could be a source of misunderstanding.
> (*Pastoral guidelines*, 2)

It should be noted that the bishops of India, like other critics, have not gone into the texts of Father de Mello quoted by the *Notification* and references made to them. Hence, the arguments of the Roman writers have not been addressed until now. Avoiding all disrespect to the teaching authority of the Congregation of the Doctrine of the Faith, they end the matter with the typical Indian attitude of paying respectful homage:
> We, the bishops of India are grateful to the Holy See for bringing certain unacceptable formulations in the writings of late Fr Tony de Mello to our notice.
> (*Pastoral guidelines*, 6)

But, at the same time, they do not betray their dear Father Tony:
> We take this opportunity to express our recognition and appreciation of the good that these writings have done to many readers, both Christians and others.
> (*Pastoral guidelines*, 6)

The reaction of the Jesuits in India

The present day Jesuit community in India, totalling over 3000, is the largest in the world if the active members are counted. Their reaction came immediately, a couple of days after the publication of the *Notification*. Father Lisbert D'Souza, the Jesuit provincial of India, said that 'the right to ban those writings of Father de Mello, which it finds to be deviating of the Christian faith, was in the rights of the Vatican' but he also added, 'I feel the relevance and spiritual insights in some of his works are closely misunderstood, because they have been published differently (by some of his followers) without his knowledge and permission.' (cf *The Tablet*, 25 September 1999) In a later declaration, the same Jesuit provincial defended Father de Mello and his works in the context of the inculturation of the Christian gospel in the modern society. In defending the theologians in Asia, who have taken this question very seriously and have been making concrete moves to realise it in present day society, he writes the following:

> Living and working amidst such challenges, we, like many of our fellow Jesuits, are pained by the atmosphere of suspicion, not to say mistrust, created by recent decisions of the Congregation for the Doctrine of the Faith about our brothers Anthony de Mello and Jacques Dupuis, which seems symptomatic of a general discouragement, even disapproval of the direction that Asian theology is taking. We think that such suspicion has been a disservice to the whole church. The late Anthony de Mello pioneered the integration of Asian and Christian spirituality and methods of prayer. He has helped thousands of people in South Asia and across the world in gaining freedom and in deepening their life of prayer, of which we have abundant testimonies and our own personal experiences.
> (Lisbert D'Souza S.J., President, Jesuit conference of South Asia, for the Jesuit Major Superiors of South Asia, 25 August, 1999).

He thanks the bishops of Asia who have taken up the support of the theologians and goes on to express the following:

> We are grateful for the appreciation and support our theologians have received from many bishops and the people of God, in Asia and the world. We invite all, bishops, clergy, and the laity, to continue to support them with a trust that is sympathetic but not naïve, critical but not censorious, be-

cause we are convinced of the importance of the theological task both for our work of evangelisation, education and social justice, and for our whole thrust towards the inculturation of our faith. We would like to assure our theologians of our own continued support and encouragement to go ahead, joyfully and in fidelity to God, to the gospel and to the church, with the difficult and challenging task of making the Word of God relevant to the situation in South Asia. (Ibid.)

The Jesuit theologian, Father Samuel Rayan, commenting on the publication, said that by banning Father de Mello's works, the Vatican was 'using sword against pen'. (cf *Eglises d'Asie*, No 270, 1 Septembre, 1998, p 8-9) According to him, what is needed most is 'a theological judgement and healthy criticism' on the objectionable writings of Father de Mello: 'Instead of declaring Father de Mello's works as incompatible with the faith and banning his books, the Vatican should have lifted the objectionable passages and properly studied them.' (Ibid.)

However, in my opinion, the Jesuits, as a whole, have not reacted sufficiently to defend and uphold their brother. To my best knowledge, their superior general in Rome has not made any declaration. In fact, in the Jesuit headquarters in Rome, there seems to have been certain hesitation with regards to Father de Mello. In 1992, I had an opportunity to be received there by one of the major Jesuit superiors. His remark that 'Tony de Mello's spirituality was not a Jesuit spirituality but a sort of Hindu-Buddhist mixture' shocked me profoundly. Even such a high-placed responsible person had not carefully read de Mello, particularly his work *Sadhana – A Way to God*, which, as Anthony de Mello understood it, was to be a newer presentation in modern times of the essence of the *Spiritual Exercises* of St Ignatius of Loyola. Furthermore, he prepared that work specifically for his Jesuit brethren. He had no intention of offering a Hindu-Buddhist mixture.

Did the Jesuits preferred to sacrifice one of their illustrious members instead of entering into conflict with the Vatican in an atmosphere that was already tense with misgivings regarding their full allegiance and obedience to the Pope? A year before the release of the *Notification*, on 11 March 1997 the Jesuits headquarters had issued a statement alerting the world about pirating false editions of Father de Mello's works. The Jesuit publisher of Father de Mello's work had stated that there were only nine authentic works, and that he regrets the publication of numerous other works under the name of Father Anthony de Mello, whose contents were partly based on his recorded conferences. These could not be attributed to him because he was very careful about reading and re-reading his manuscripts before they went to the press. The Vatican authorities apparently did not judge this warning as a sufficient explanation nor did they deem it necessary to investigate it in order to sift the weeds from the corn.

My efforts in India to assess the Jesuit reaction have not yielded much result. I got the impression that Tony de Mello's message and teachings, taken very seriously during his lifetime, were being given up in order to re-emphasise the old routine and the old form of the *Spiritual Exercises*. When I discussed the matter with the Jesuit Provincial in Delhi, Father Lisbert D'Souza, he gave me two reasons for this apparent apathy. First, he said that one felt helpless before the Vatican authorities, who somehow or other do not understand from Rome what happens in the distant Indies. Secondly, Tony was such a unique stalwart with such unique charisma that there was no one among them to equal him. That was apparently the reason why the Sadhana Institute, founded by him in Lonavla, has now been turned into a psychological institute for training and for issuing diplomas.

Reactions over the World
The reactions outside India and outside the Jesuit order were also numerous. Practically every religious newspaper reported on the *Notification*. But many of them just exposed the main points raised by Rome without entering into the matters about which the warning was issued. It was evident that people did not really know who Anthony de Mello was and why the Vatican was issuing a warning. Even theologians, like my colleagues at the Faculties of Theology in Fribourg and Neuchâtel (Switzerland), were incapable of commenting on the matter since none of them seem to have read de Mello. Apparently the titles and the presentation of his books in French and German

appeared to them to be too popular to be intellectually nourishing. However, there have been some interesting comments coming from different sources, and I have had the chance of stumbling upon a few of them.

The study of a Czech theologian, Ivana Dolejsová, *When a Bird Sings* ... is full of deep intuitions. She notes pointedly: '... the *Notification* attempts to 'explain' de Mello's metaphorical language, but in fact turns it into literal descriptions and thus destroys it. The question I want to conclude with is: Which authentic theological impulses underlie the *Notification*?' (cf *The Month*, January 1999, p 17).

Father Billy Hewett SJ, the renowned spiritual guide in England for the *Spiritual Exercises* and a good friend of Tony, writes a strong plea for *Sadhana – A Way to God*. His article 'Within the lines' (cf *The Month*, January 1999) points out the solid orthodoxy of Father de Mello's spirituality and makes a clear assessment of the Roman *Notification*:

> The documents issued by the Congregation of Rights contain objectively erroneous misinterpretations of what de Mello actually wrote and taught. Simply to blame and pillory with cynical or even self-righteous remarks does not help. To expect an immediate apology and correction is unrealistic. Roman congregations seldom act that way (cf Galileo or Teilhard de Chardin to name but two). But since in fact the blanket condemnation can be shown not to be appropriate in the case of sadhana, loyal and committed Roman Catholics should be able to continue to be both loyal and committed and free to practice sadhana.
> (*The Month*, January 1999, 23)

'*Anthony de Mello en el punto de mira*' (*Vida Nueva*, 3 de octobre de 1998) is another interesting article which sums up the reactions of certain Spanish theologians to the Roman *Notification*. The author, theologian J. Fernándes states that the religious people consulted for *Vida Nueva* massively express their objection to the *Notification*, not because they refuse to admit difficulties in de Mello's teachings, but that his work should be seen more globally. The blame frequently addressed is that the immense help brought by Father de Mello to numerous people and the good done by him is not taken into consideration. Quoting a person who wants to remain anonymous, the author writes:

> De Mello has done good around him and has brought many people closer to God. Why is this not taken into account? In my opinion, that is absolutely essential. If we go through spiritual books with a magnifying glass in hand, including some written by saints, we will obtain similar results. It should be remembered that de Mello was not a theologian, he did not try to theologise; he was a writer, a guide. (p 25)

The article notes that this *Notification* is not a condemnation but a warning and therefore 'we should take it as a plea to Christian maturity to read de Mello with a sense of critique; but it is regrettable to devalue the good de Mello has done.' (Ibid.)

The Spanish theologian sees this document as a preamble to the Encyclical Letter *Fides et Ratio* (14 September 1998) and related to the recent Synod of the Asian bishops, where many complained about the insufficient inculturation of the gospel in Asia: 'Numerous participants in the Synod expressed their surprise at the fact that Jesus Christ, a true Asiatic, should be still presented in Asia as an 'imported foreigner'. He needs to be proclaimed, as does Anthony de Mello, with a new pastoral approach, projecting first the image of man, prophet, saviour and source of freedom who is also full of compassion. Only then can we proclaim his divine Sonship, which is an unfathomable mystery even for the most sublime theology.' (Ibid.)

Another renowned theologian of Salamanca, who admits that he has not read de Mello, notes, however, that the *Notification* needs to take into consideration cultural difficulties in spreading the gospel. Problems like inculturation in Asia, particularly in India, the dialogue with Hinduism and Buddhism, the relationship of these religions with Christianity and the important questions like the confrontation of revealed religion with the human conscience open to the Absolute, Jesus Christ as the Saviour etc. Clearly, the *Notification* has not undertaken such an endeavour. Furthermore, he adds: 'De Mello did not have a dogmatic purpose. He was a narrator. The gospels, too, are narrations. All the narrations rest upon presuppositions, which are not explicit. That is why these narrations have been helpful to so many.' (Ibid.)

One thing can be said in conclusion: no applause has been given to the *Notification*. Many have accepted it through the habitual obedience they show to the church authorities, but none has come forward with comments supporting the Roman writers.

Father Carlos Vallés
Father Carlos Vallés (+1925), a Spanish Jesuit priest who lived in India and worked there as professor of mathematics, has stepped into this controversy. Vallés has authored many books and articles of spiritual interest in his mother tongue Spanish, but also in English and in the Indian Gujarati language, which was his major work language for the more than forty years he spent in India. He is back now in his native Madrid, from where he continues to publish and conduct various seminars over the world.

Carlos Vallés met Anthony de Mello in India in the context of sadhana and from then on became his great admirer and friend. Soon after de Mello's death, he published his *Unencumbered by baggage. Anthony de Mello – a prophet for our times* (Gujarat Sahitya Prakash, Anand, 1987). The book was published barely a month after Tony's death. It is not a biography of Tony but presents Tony as a spiritual master and conductor of sadhanas, the way in which Carlos perceived him in admiration. The contents are all the more interesting because they were, as Vallés attests in the book, the notes taken down during the last sadhana Tony gave in April 1987, and Carlos took them down under the premonition he had that that sadhana was going to be Tony's last!

> I got an uncanny feeling, a definite premonition or foreboding that Tony was going to die after the Renewal, and that this last course was going to be his spiritual testament to us.
> (*Unencumbered by Baggage*, 6)

The book is full of praise and admiration of Anthony de Mello. The dedication reads: 'Thanking you, TONY, master and friend.' Vallés resumés Tony's teachings very well, although some of his fundamental spiritual concepts seem to be missing, for example, Tony's teaching about the 'I,' 'Not-I,' 'Life after death,' 'attachment and detachment'. Reading this book one gets the impression that the author had taken very seriously to heart what he claims having heard from Tony – that he was the only person who had really understood him.

But ten years after this work he comes out with another work, *Diez Anos Despues. Reflexiones sobre Anthony de Mello*, (1998 Editorial San Pablo), in which he makes a complete about face towards his master and friend. The book is not translated into English. Probably the author knows that it would pain and distress thousands of readers and admirers of Tony in India and elsewhere. As I do not read Spanish, I read it in its German translation, *Nachdenken über Anthony de Mello* (2001 Santiago Verlag, Asperheide 88, D-47574 Goch). It makes for a sickening reading because the book is not really on de Mello but on the perception of Carlos Vallés (and exclusively his own) of Anthony de Mello. It is full of 'I' and 'me', not in the sense of Tony's teachings but referring to the author's person. The praise and admiration for Tony has disappeared. The author gives vent to his own pain suffered under the weight of Tony's international fame and reputation.

To whom is Father de Mello a danger?
I think I have sufficiently shown from the above analysis that Father de Mello, far from being a danger to the Catholic faith, is, on the contrary, a prophetic and mystical teacher whose works have brought immense help to a vast number of people and continue to do so. After his death, his authentic books continue to bring much light and consolation in accordance with the teachings of the church.

The greatest contribution of Father de Mello is that he is one of the rare spiritual masters who know to speak to the modern world in which over eighty percent of the population has given up the regular practice of their faith in the church or to abide by its teachings. One of the reasons for this distancing from the church is the fact that they do not understand its language even when she speaks in their own mother-tongue. Many contemporary Christians, who have consciously or unconsciously distanced from the church, are not basically hostile to the Christian message. They simply refuse to accept it the way it is preached by the church through its institutions. De Mello brings a new taste and flavour to the Christian message. He makes God an adventurous experience and preaches a return to the 'Abba-Father' experience of Jesus of the gospels. The church which he preaches is the one in which the faithful worship 'the Father in spirit and truth'. (John 4:23)

A Prophet for our times
Like the prophets of the Old Testament and also like the Prophet of the New Testament, Jesus of Nazareth, Father de Mello is a disturbing element in the establishment. It is further known in the study of religions that a prophet gets into conflicts first with the religious leaders. These have the task of overseeing the good of not only a few of their flocks but the good of all. They have also the responsibility of maintaining smooth relationships with the social and political establishments. History shows that religions work out compromises and adapt their teachings for a so-called peace which is not always compatible with the message of their founders. It is the prophet who is free and unbound that comes on the scene to shake up everyone, provoking a creative disorder that makes everyone really think and then return to the founding spirit. The prophet's action is motivated by love and concern. However, the religious authorities often do not see it that way.

Father de Mello: A Healer
The prophetic action of Father de Mello had, in the first place, a healing effect on many. If he took up religious concepts and themes in his teachings, it was not for a theological or academic debate but essentially for a healing: for freeing people from fear and anguish in order to lighten their burden created through imaginary and structural conditions and to give people a taste for life and the joy of living. Father de Mello did not strive to bring back Jesuits or other religious people to the ideals of their orders. He simply sought to make people whole and healthy, first at their existential level, which was an absolute condition for building a healthy spirituality.

This healing ministry also had an indirect healing effect on the social and religious structures. Spirituality, according to de Mello, was based on the common ground of human existence and, therefore, could not be strictly limited to a set of people and cultures. A good spirituality would not separate people but would unite all. De Mello's spiritual method made people come out of their protective shells and praise God in unison. A healthy spirituality brings good health to all, not just to Catholics.

Father de Mello and the future of the Catholic Church
Father de Mello is not a danger to the Catholic faith. He invited his listeners and invites his readers into a deeper renewal of their Catholic Faith, too often experienced under 'bushels' that do not radiate light. Many in the world do not experience its strength and vitality. They live it as a routine. Others are fed up with it and go away from it, seeking their truth elsewhere. Father de Mello was extremely sensitive to this problem and, therefore, endeavoured to make the Christian life an adventurous experience. He spoke of the direct experience of God, prayer as a delicious moment of intimacy with God in all places and times, faith as a celebration of love and joy, liberating human persons and giving them a taste of the freedom of the children of God.

It would surely be a misfortune for the Catholic Church and for the world to lose this 'fire-maker' from the East. 'He was a burning and shining lamp.' (John 5:35)